NAOKI URASAWA'S

20th CENTURY BOYS

Naoki Urasawa's
20th Century Boys
Volume 02

VIZ Signature Edition

STORY AND ART BY NAOKI URASAWA

English Adaptation/Akemi Wegmüller
Touch-up Art & Lettering/Freeman Wong
Cover & Interior Design/Sam Elzway
Editor/Kit Fox

Editor in Chief, Books/Alvin Lu
Editor in Chief, Magazines/Marc Weidenbaum
VP, Publishing Licensing/Rika Inouye
VP, Sales & Product Marketing/Gonzalo Ferreyra
VP, Creative/Linda Espinosa
Publisher/Hyoe Narita

Printed in the U.S.A.

Published by VIZ Media, LLC
P.O. Box 77010
San Francisco, CA 94107

VIZ Signature Edition
10 9 8 7 6 5 4 3 2 1
First printing, April 2009

www.viz.com
store.viz.com

NAOKI URASAWA'S

20th CENTURY BOYS

VOL 02
THE PROPHET

Story & Art by
NAOKI URASAWA

With the cooperation of
Takashi NAGASAKI

NAOKI URASAWA'S 20th CENTURY BOYS

PROFILES

The Friend and his mysterious organization have begun counting down to Doomsday...and Kenji is becoming aware of their terrible plot. What will come at century's end—destruction or salvation? These are the people who hold the world's destiny in their hands!

Kanna

Daughter of Kenji's elder sister Kiriko. Father unknown. Being raised by Kenji.

↑Maruo as a kid

Maruo

Close friend of Kenji's who owns a fancy goods shop in the neighborhood. A cheerful glutton.

↑Yoshitsune as a kid

Yoshitsune

A friend of Kenji's since childhood. As a salaryman, he remains timid and inconspicuous.

Kenji

Protagonist of this story. As a child, he dreamed of becoming a hero who would one day defend the earth and bring about peace. In reality, though, he's a somewhat boring middle-aged man who owns a convenience store with his mother. Triggered by Donkey's mysterious death, he's now on a search for the "Friend."

↑Kenji as a kid

Yukiji

The mightiest tomboy. Now a customs officer, she works as a narcotics investigator in the company of a incompetent dog.

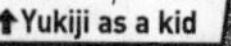

↑Yukiji as a kid

Donkey

Kenji's childhood friend. Grew up in a poor household and was a very fast runner. Donkey became a high school teacher but died a mysterious death.

↑Donkey as a kid

Otcho

Kenji's childhood friend, in many ways Otcho was the brains of their group. His job at a Japanese trading company sent him overseas, but...

↑Otcho as a kid

Kamisama ("God")

Homeless man who is worshipped by his companions. Possesses an uncanny ability to foresee future events.

Friend

A cult leader who speaks of apocalyptic prophecies. There is suspicion that he might be one of Kenji's childhood friends.

Manjome Inshu

A top executive in the Friend's organization.

Yanbo & Mabo

Kenji and his friends have known them since childhood. A pair of bullies who were called "the evilest twins in history."

Kiriko

Kenji's elder sister. Deposited infant daughter Kanna at her mother's and was never seen again.

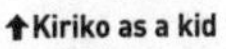

↑Kiriko as a kid

CONTENTS

VOL 02
THE PROPHET

Chap 1: "Amiability" 7

Chap 2: Otcho 25

Chap 3: Cho-san 43

Chap 4: Yama-san 61

Chap 5: Humanity's Final Hour 79

Chap 6: Kamisama 97

Chap 7: Kiriko's Desk Drawer 115

Chap 8: Kiriko's Boyfriend 135

Chap 9: The Man Behind 153

Chap 10: The Prophet 171

Chap 11: Open Your Eyes!! 189

NAOKI URASAWA'S

20th CENTURY BOYS

Chapter 1 "Amiability"

BWUMFGH!!

KA-THUNK

!!

THERE WAS ONE PERSON, AND ONE PERSON ONLY...

WHO D'YA THINK YOU'RE MESSIN' WITH, YOU!!

...WHO COULD BEAT THE CRAP OUT OF THEM...

GWAP

WARGH!!

THWOK

GWUMPH!!

AND SHE WAS SOME-THING ELSE!!
PICK ON TANABE-KUN AGAIN AND I'M NOT LETTING YOU GET AWAY WITH IT!!

WHO SAYS WE WERE PICKING ON HIM?
I WOULDN'T GO AROUND MAKING ***FALSE ACCUSA-TIONS*** IF I WERE--

ZWAP
GYARGH!!

OWWWOWOWOWOW!!
GYEE GYEE
DON'T PLAY DUMB WITH ME...

OKAY ?!
ZUMP!
BWORGH!!

HUMPH!!
YOU'LL BE SORRY FOR THIS, ***STUPID!!***

THE STRONGEST GIRL THAT EVER LIVED, YUKIJI!!

Chapter 1
"Amiability"

*New Tokyo International Airport

IT'S YUKIJI, YOU GUYS!!
I RECOGNIZED YOU RIGHT AWAY!!
YOU HAVEN'T CHANGED A BIT, GIRL!! REALLY!!
...

HAVEN'T... CHANGED ?!
NOT EVEN... A BIT?!

WE HEARD ALL ABOUT YOU LATER IN JUNIOR HIGH! YOUR HEROIC FEATS WERE LEGENDARY!!
EH ?!

TOOK ON THE BADDEST GANG AT NO. 6 JUNIOR HIGH, 13 GUYS, OUT ON THE RIVERBANK!!
SENT ALL 13 OF THEM STRAIGHT TO THE HOSPITAL! WHEN WE HEARD THAT WE SAID, "THAT'S OUR YUKIJI!!" RIGHT, GUYS?!

THAT... GOT KINDA BLOWN UP!!
THERE WERE ONLY 12 OF THEM ...

THEN IN HIGH SCHOOL, BATTLE ROYALE WITH THE MOTOR-CYCLE GANG!!
HEH ?!

YOU STRIPPED THEIR BOSS BUCK-NAKED AND TRUSSED HIM UP, RIGHT?!
WELL... ACTUALLY, HE STILL HAD ON HIS UNDER-PANTS...

CANINE TEAM
A PRO... WRESTLER? WAIT A MINUTE, WHO'S BEEN SPREADING THESE LIES ABOUT ME?!

AND THEN AFTER THAT WE HEARD YOU BECAME A PRO WRESTLER!
HUH ?!
WISH WE COULD'VE SEEN YOU! IS IT TRUE YOU NEVER LOST A SINGLE FIGHT?

AND NOW LOOK AT HER, A FULL-ON NARC! WOW!!
...
THAT'S OUR YUKIJI FOR YOU, HUH?!!

REMEMBER? YUKIJI'S GRAND-DAD WAS A BONESETTER, AND HALF HIS PATIENTS HAD THEIR BONES BROKEN BY YUKIJI! HE WAS DOING A ROARING TRADE!!
GOTTA GET OUT OF HERE !!

I AM NOT A NARC, OKAY ?!
I'M JUST AN ORDINARY CUSTOMS OFFICER AND--
REGIONAL
CANINE TEAM

IF I DON'T ESCAPE THIS DARK PAST, I HAVE NO FUTURE!!
COME ON, BLUE THREE !!

SHAA SHAA
ARGH, BLUE THREE, WE'RE *GOING* !!
UH... HEY, WAIT! YUKIJI!!

THIS... STUPID POOCH IS NAMED BRUCE LEE?!
HANH
BLUE, THE COLOR, THREE, THE NUMBER !!

SHAA SHAA SHAA
SORRY! I'M REALLY BUSY!!

GIVE US YOUR NUMBER! LET'S ALL GO OUT SOMETIME!!
SOUNDS GOOD. I LIKE THAT!! SOUNDS GREAT.
YOU'RE BLUSHING AGAIN, YOSHITSUNE. WHAT'S THIS ALL ABOUT?

CUSTOMS
TEAM

HANG OUT WITH THIS BUNCH AND I'LL NEVER FIND A HUSBAND!!
YUKIJIII !!

HANG ON, YUKIJI!!
DO YOU RECOG-NIZE THIS SYMBOL ?!

...

CAN YOU REMEMBER SOMETHING? ANYTHING AT ALL?!
LIKE, WHO ELSE KNEW IT OR WHO WAS THE ONE WHO CAME UP WITH IT?!

GOOD-BYE! I'M REALLY BUSY!!

YUKIJI ...
WHAT'S WITH *HER?*
...

SHAA
SHA
SHA

Blondy
ICHIHARA SETSUKO, ATTORNEY-AT-LAW...
Nakatsugawa Law Firm
Ichihara Setsuko
Attorney-at-law
Hitotsubashi, Chiyoda-ku, Tokyo
Tel: 3230-54XX
Fax: 5210-76XX

YES, I'M AN ATTORNEY WITH THE NAKATSUGAWA LAW FIRM. PLEASED TO MEET YOU.
AND MY NAME IS NIIKURA. I'M ALSO AN ATTORNEY.

THANK YOU FOR TAKING THIS TIME OUT OF YOUR BUSY SCHEDULE. AS I SAID WHEN WE SPOKE ON THE PHONE...

KACHAK KACHAK
HERE YOU ARE.

CHAK

AS I SAID OVER THE PHONE, OUR OFFICE HAS RECEIVED NUMEROUS INQUIRIES FROM PEOPLE WHOSE CHILDREN ARE INVOLVED IN YOUR ORGANIZATION.
THESE PARENTS ARE REQUESTING OUR HELP IN RECLAIMING THEIR SONS AND DAUGHTERS.

KLAK

WHAT DO YOU HAVE TO SAY IN THIS REGARD?

KLINK KLINK

INSHU ...

IF WE CANNOT GET A CLEAR ANSWER FROM YOU, WE WILL BE FORCED TO TAKE THE NECESSARY STEPS, MR.... MANJOME?

MANJOME INSHU.
A DIFFICULT NAME TO READ, I KNOW. MY APOLOGIES.

SPEAKING OF "DIFFICULT TO READ," YOUR GROUP'S NAME...

WHAT IS IT, EXACTLY?

NAME?

YES, NAME. YOU NEED ONE, DON'T YOU?

WHY DO WE NEED A NAME?

CERTAINLY AN ORGANIZATION NEEDS A NAME IF IT'S TO BE RECOGNIZED BY SOCIETY.

LOOK HERE, MS. ICHI-HARA.
IF YOU INSIST ON HAVING A NAME FOR US...

TOK TOK
THIS IS OUR NAME.

...

THIS "FRIEND" WHO IS THE PURPORTED LEADER OF YOUR GROUP...
CAN YOU TELL US HIS NAME, THEN?

OUR FRIEND IS...
SIMPLY OUR FRIEND.

ARE YOU SAYING YOU WILL NOT REVEAL ANY NAMES WHAT-SOEVER?

LOOK HERE, MS. ICHI-HARA.

OUR FRIEND DOES NOT, IN ANY WAY, RESTRAIN OR CONFINE THOSE WHO COME SEEKING HIS FRIENDSHIP.
ALL THESE PEOPLE ARE DOING IS, QUITE SIMPLY, GATHERING AROUND THEIR FRIEND. THAT IS ALL.

SO WHO IS THIS "FRIEND" OF YOURS, THEN?

HE IS SOMEONE WHO POSSESSES GREAT AMIABILITY.

AMIABI-LITY?

HE IS THE ONLY BEING PERMITTED TO USE THIS...
TOK

...AND THE FIRST BEING EVER TO HAVE CONCEIVED THIS.
TOK

DO YOU UNDERSTAND, MS. ICHIHARA?

?

WELL THEN, I MUST GO...

UH... PLEASE WAIT A MOMENT!!

WHAT'S THE MATTER WITH HIM?
HMMM... WHERE DID I SEE HIM BEFORE ...

WHAT?

THAT MAN-JOME ...
I THINK I'VE SEEN HIM SOME-WHERE ...

WELL, I HAVE TO SAY, HE'S A SHADY CHARACTER STRAIGHT FROM CENTRAL CASTING...

?!

N-NIIKU-RA!!
WHA--!! WHAT'S THE MATTER, MS. ICHIHARA?!

L-LOOK!!
GYAK!!

THE SPOONS... ARE ALL...!!

酒
*Liquor

FWAAAH.
...

THWOK
OOLONG
OOLONG
TEA
JAM
BEAN BUN

UH... GOOD DAY TO...

HEY...

HMM. SO YOU AREN'T A LIQUOR STORE ANY-MORE.

YUKI-JI...

YOU KNOW THAT SYMBOL YOU SHOWED ME?

IT CAME BACK TO ME.
I REMEMBER WHO CAME UP WITH IT.

YOU DO? WHO?

Chapter 2 Otcho

I JUST CAN'T BELIEVE THAT GUY WOULD COMMIT SUICIDE...
THAT'S... SEE, I THINK MAYBE IT ***WASN'T*** A SUICIDE!!

I SAW IT IN THE PAPER.

HE SENT ME A LETTER. RIGHT BEFORE HE DIED...

...
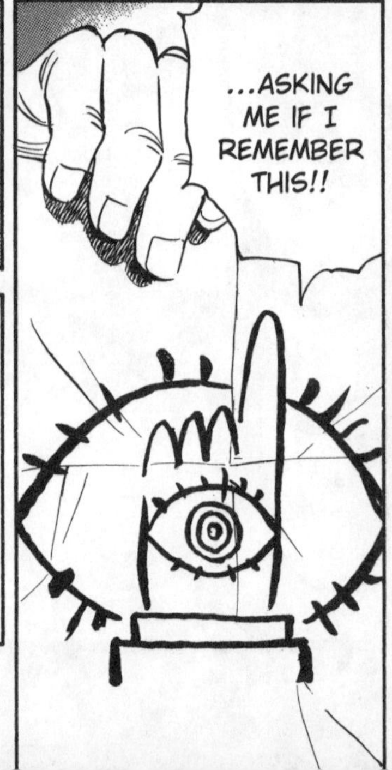
...ASKING ME IF I REMEMBER THIS!!

IT'S POSSIBLE THAT DONKEY GOT INTO SOME KIND OF TROUBLE BECAUSE OF THIS SYMBOL!!
SO IF YOU REMEMBER, YOU GOTTA TELL ME, YUKIJI!!

WHO INVENTED THIS? WHO WAS IT?!
IT WAS OTCHO.
OTCHO ...
WHOOSH
LET'S MAKE A SECRET EMBLEM.
THIS SYMBOL IS OUR GANG'S EMBLEM!!

WHOOSH
IF YOU KNOW THIS SYMBOL, YOU'RE A REAL FRIEND.
Chapter 2
Otcho

HA HA HA!
SO IT WAS OTCHO ...

YOU'RE RIGHT... I REMEMBER!
IT WAS OTCHO!!

WELCOME TO KING MART!!
!!

GOOD DAY TO YOU, YOUNG LADIES!!
OH...

MISTER ENDO ...
LET'S GREET OUR CUSTOMERS!!

UH... YESSIR ...
WHO'S THAT?

HE'S FROM KING MART HEADQUARTERS. HE'S THE SALES GUY IN CHARGE OF THIS DISTRICT AND...
OH YEAH, HE'S THE FRANCHISE COP.

WELL, I'M OFF, THEN.
UH... YUKIJI, WAIT...

MR. ENDO!! I'VE BEEN WATCHING YOU AND IT SEEMS TO ME YOU THINK OF THE CASH REGISTER AS A PLACE TO STAND AROUND GOSSIPING.
UH... NO...

KENJI.
I CAME BECAUSE YOU SEEMED TO BE SERIOUS ABOUT WANTING TO GET TO THE BOTTOM OF THIS. HERE. GO TO THIS LAW FIRM!

A FRIEND OF MINE NAMED ICHIHARA WORKS THERE.
THEY'RE HOLDING A MEETING TODAY AT TWO, TO REPORT THEIR FINDINGS ON THE "FRIEND" GROUP TO VICTIMS.

YEAH, BUT... I...
AHEM!!
Ichihara Setsuko

WHAT WOULD I DO THERE?
I DON'T SEE WHAT'S THE USE OF ME--

JUST TELL THEM EVERYTHING YOU KNOW.
I'M SURE YOUR TESTIMONY WILL HELP THEM A LOT.

THE GROUP WE'RE DEALING WITH SOUNDS PRETTY SINISTER ...
BUT I KNOW YOU'LL DO IT ANYWAY.

THAT'S WHY I'M HERE. BECAUSE I KNEW YOU WOULD.

BYE!!
UH... YUKIJI ...

AHEM!!
!!

MR. ENDO. I'D LIKE A WORD.

UH... YESSIR.

YUKI-JI...
THE STRONGEST GIRL THAT EVER LIVED...

TORYAAAA!!
THUNK

GET UP, YANBO! MABO! LET'S SEE YOU FIGHT FAIR FOR A CHANGE!!
YOU BULLIES! I CAN'T STAND BULLIES!!

NGH... SCREW YOU, YOU... MAN-GIRL!!
MAN-GIRL!!

I SAID, GET UP AND FIGHT FAIR!! ALWAYS PICKING ON KIDS WHO'RE WEAKER THAN YOU...
HOW ABOUT FIGHTING SOMEONE STRONGER, YOU BIG COWARDS ?!

URRRGH!!
MUMBLE MUMBLE

HAH !!
RIGHT ?!

HMPH !!
WHAT, YOU WANT ME TO BEAT YOU UP AGAIN?!

YOU'RE THE ONE WHO'S NO FAIR, YUKIJI!
NO FAIR, YUKIJI!

I ALWAYS FIGHT FAIR!!

NO, YOU DON'T. IT'S NOT SUMO IF YOU GRAB SOMEONE'S SLEEVE TO THROW 'EM.
OR THEIR COLLAR. CHEATER!

WHAT'S WRONG WITH THAT?!

FWAP
YOU GOTTA BE NAKED TO DO SUMO!!
THAT'S RIGHT! PLAY FAIR AND TAKE OFF YOUR CLOTHES!!

UH-OH, WHAT'S THE MAAATTER?
TAKE 'EM OFF, COME ONNNN!
FLUBBER FLUBBER
FLUBBER FLUBBER

UH-OH, WHAT'S THE MATTER? SHE CAN'T TAKE 'EM OFF?
THAT'S TOO BAD. SO I GUESS SHE LOST, THEN?

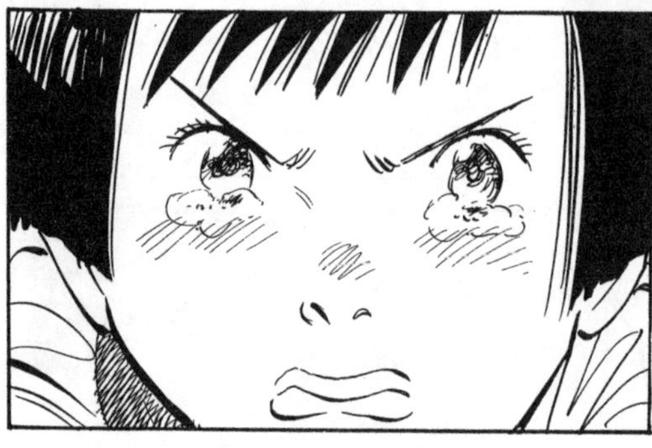

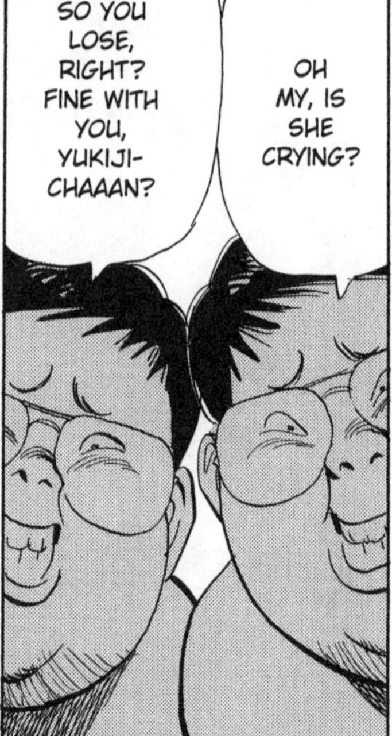
OH MY, IS SHE CRYING?
SO YOU LOSE, RIGHT? FINE WITH YOU, YUKIJI-CHAAAN?

TAKE-- THEM-- OFF--
COME ONNN, HURRY UUUUP.

WHAT'S THE PROBLEM?!
JUST TAKE 'EM OFF!!

YOU CAN'T DO IT YOURSELF, WE'LL DO IT FOR YA.
LET'S GO, COME ON!!
STOP IT!!

HWUH?

NNNGG-HRAAA-ARGH!!
SHWA

KENJI ...

...

TOK
TOK
SORRY I'M LATE, YUKIJI.
OH... NO BIGGIE.

A LOT OF PEOPLE SHOWED UP FOR THIS VICTIMS' GROUP OF YOURS...
I KNOW.

HUB
BUB
AND ALL OF THEM HAVE LOST SONS AND DAUGHTERS TO THAT WEIRD "FRIEND" CULT.

THEY'RE HERE BECAUSE THEY WANT TO GET THEM BACK...

DID YOU FIND OUT... ABOUT OTCHO?

HEY THANKS, YUKIJI--FOR HELPING ME OUT WITH THIS.
WHO'D HAVE GUESSED, HUH, THAT SOMEONE YOU GREW UP WITH INVENTED THIS SYMBOL...

OCHIAI CHOJI ...
INTEREST-INGLY ENOUGH, PRESENT WHERE-ABOUTS UNKNOWN ...

...

HERE. IT'S A NEWS-PAPER ARTICLE FROM NINE YEARS AGO.

Japanese trading company man goes missing in Thailand.
Met with road accident in jungle?
THIS MISSING TRADING COMPANY MAN IS YOUR OLD BUDDY OTCHO.

HE'S BEEN MISSING EVER SINCE?

UH-UH. THAT TIME, THEY FOUND HIM A WEEK LATER.
BUT IT WAS NEVER REPORTED WHAT HAPPENED TO HIM DURING THAT WEEK.

HE QUIT HIS JOB RIGHT AFTER THIS...
AND...HE HAD A WIFE AND CHILD HERE IN JAPAN, BUT ABOUT A MONTH BEFORE THIS INCIDENT, THEY GOT DIVORCED.

WHAT DID HE DO AFTER HE QUIT?

THE TRAIL GOES COLD AFTER THAT.
I HAVE TO SAY, IT'S PRETTY SUSPICIOUS.

YEAH, BUT...
...I CAN'T BELIEVE OTCHO WOULD ...

WHOOPS, IT'S TIME.
OH...THAT KENJI I MENTIONED. DID YOU HEAR FROM HIM?

UH-UH, NOT YET.
OH...

BUT HE'LL BE HERE, RIGHT?

IT WOULD BE SO HELPFUL IF HE COULD TELL EVERYONE WHAT HE KNOWS!!

HE'LL COME.
I'M POSI-TIVE!

HUB BUB
SORRY TO HAVE KEPT YOU WAITING, LADIES AND GENTLEMEN!!

YOU'RE COMING, KENJI...

I KNOW IT. REMEMBER THAT TIME?

酒
LOOK AT THIS, MR. ENDO! TAKE A GOOD LOOK AT THESE LATE-NIGHT SALES FIGURES!!
THIS IS HALF OF WHAT YOUR COMPETITION'S MAKING, 200 METERS DOWN THE STREET. HALF!!
*Liquor

THE TOBACCONIST ON THE CORNER'S TALKING ABOUT JOINING THE FRANCHISE!!
IF YOUR SALES FIGURES STAY AT THIS LEVEL, WE MAY CHOOSE TO CANCEL OUR CONTRACT WITH YOU!!

UH... UH-HUH.

THAT TIME, YOU KNEW YOU DIDN'T STAND A CHANCE AGAINST THOSE TWO, BUT YOU LAUNCHED YOURSELF AT THEM ANYWAY...

AND OF COURSE, THEY BEAT YOU TO A PULP... BUT...

...AS I SAT THERE BLUBBER-ING, YOU SAID...
DON'T CRY, YUKIJI ...

JOIN OUR GANG AND FIGHT EVIL WITH US.

...

YOU NEED TO GET YOUR ACT TOGETHER, MR. ENDO!!
CIVILIAN
YUKIJI ...

THE GUY I AM TODAY ...
...IS NOT THE GUY I WAS BACK THEN...
...

Chapter 3
Cho-san

PIKACHU?
WHAT'S THAT?

...YEAH? A MONSTER IN SOME ANIME SERIES?
IS THAT WHAT'S POPULAR WITH KIDS THESE DAYS?

WELL, I'M NOT EXACTLY ON TOP OF STUFF LIKE THAT...
UH-HUH. PIKACHU, WAS IT? I'LL LOOK FOR IT.

WELL, THEN ...
UM... CHO-SAN?

HAVE YOU THOUGHT ABOUT WHAT I SAID THE OTHER DAY?

UH...YEAH. BUT, WELL, GRATEFUL AS I AM TO YOU, HIROYUKI...
COME LIVE WITH US.

THANKS, HIROYUKI, BUT I REALLY DON'T THINK MY DAUGHTER WANTS ME IN HER HOUSE.
PLEASE, JUST MEET WITH YUMIKO ONCE TO TALK IT OVER...

LOOK... I'VE GOTTEN USED TO LIVING ALONE LIKE THIS. YOU DON'T HAVE TO WORRY ABOUT ME.
CHO-SAN ...
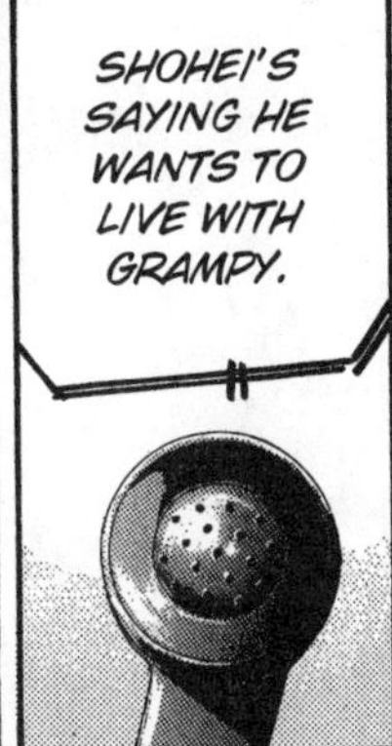
SHOHEI'S SAYING HE WANTS TO LIVE WITH GRAMPY.

...

TELL SHOHEI-CHAN TO LOOK FORWARD TO HIS BIRTHDAY PRESENT FROM ME, WILL YOU?
UH... CHO-SAN ...

KLIK

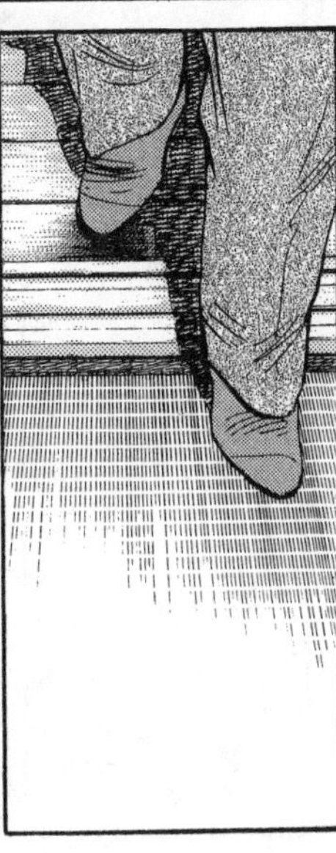

*Police Station
*Traffic Safety

HEY, YAMA-SAN.
WHAT YOU GOT IN THAT BAG?

PIKACHU.

PIKA-CHU?

WHAT, YOU DON'T KNOW IT? IT'S ALL THE RAGE AMONG THE KIDS RIGHT NOW.
HUH. THAT'S OUR CHO-SAN, ALWAYS ON TOP OF THINGS.

US GUM-SHOES GOTTA STICK OUR NOSES IN EVERYTHING, Y'KNOW?

YOU'RE ABSOLUTELY RIGHT ABOUT THAT.

HEY YAMA-SAN, GOOD I BUMPED INTO YOU. GOT A FEW MINUTES?

Peanut
CAFE Peanuts
ピーナッツ

WE'RE REALLY GONNA MISS YOU...

HM?

YOUR RETIRE-MENT'S COMING UP SOON.

YOU'LL ALL BE GLAD TO GET RID OF ME.
HECK NO... THE THOUGHT THAT IN A WEEK'S TIME WE WON'T BE HEARING YOU YELLING AT US ANY-MORE...
TOY TOY

A WEEK... WELL, THAT'S WHAT I WANTED TO TALK TO YOU ABOUT...

HUH?
THERE'S NO WAY IN HELL THIS CASE IS GONNA BE SEWN UP IN A WEEK'S TIME, SEE. I WANT YOU TO TAKE IT OVER FOR ME, YAMA-SAN.

UH-HUH...
THE SHIKISHIMA CASE. YOU KNOW, THE OCHANOMIZU PROFESSOR...

THE ONE WHERE THE WHOLE FAMILY'S GONE MISSING?
YEAH...

BY THE WAY, YAMA-SAN. THE CASE YOU'RE WORKING ON, THAT STUDENT WHO DIED HEMORRHAGING ALL OVER HIS BODY...
SHIKISHIMA WAS HIS ADVISOR. YOU GET THE AUTOPSY REPORT?

OH, THAT...
THAT CASE IS NO LONGER POLICE BUSINESS. IT'S OUT OF OUR HANDS.

MEAN-ING?

THE VIRAL RESEARCH LAB AT TOKYO UNIVERSITY'S ANALYZING THE BLOOD SAMPLES AND CARRYING OUT A WHOLE BUNCH OF TESTS. THAT WAS NO CRIME, CHO-SAN, IT WAS A DISEASE.
A DISEASE?

THE SYMPTOMS ARE ALMOST IDENTICAL TO THAT CONTAGIOUS DISEASE THAT BROKE OUT IN AFRICA.

PLUS, WE FOUND OUT THE STUDENT HAD BEEN TRAVELING IN AFRICA RIGHT BEFORE HE DIED, SO...

HMM... HAVE THEY IDENTIFIED THE VIRUS?

TELL YOU THE TRUTH, I DON'T KNOW. LIKE I SAID, IT'S OUT OF MY HANDS.

THOUGH I'M JUMPY AS HELL RIGHT NOW, WONDERING IF I GOT INFECTED MYSELF. THE GUY'S BLOOD WAS EVERY-WHERE.

I'M TELLING YOU, THAT ONE'S FOR THE HEALTH AUTHORI-TIES...
LET *THEM* FREAK OUT ABOUT IT. IT'S NOT A CRIMINAL CASE, CHO-SAN, BELIEVE ME!

...

IT'S TRUE THE TWO CASES LOOKED LIKE THEY WERE RELATED, COMING RIGHT ON TOP OF EACH OTHER LIKE THAT AND WITH SHIKISHIMA TURNING OUT TO BE THE KID'S ADVISOR. I THOUGHT SO MYSELF, WHICH IS WHY I DISCUSSED IT WITH YOU, CHO-SAN. BUT IF THE GUY WENT TO AFRICA AND BROUGHT BACK A DEADLY DISEASE, THAT'S A WHOLE DIFFERENT BALLGAME.
I THINK THE SHIKISHIMA ANGLE'S JUST A COINCIDENCE. A STRANGE COINCIDENCE, MAYBE, BUT NOTHING MORE THAN THAT.

NOT A CRIMINAL CASE... HMM.
HUH?

OR MAYBE IT'S A CASE SO HUGE IT'LL BLOW US OUT OF THE WATER.

WHAT DO YOU MEAN?

CRAZY TIMES, AFTER ALL... WE COULD BE DEALING WITH BIOLOGICAL WEAPONS.

COME ON...
TAKE A LOOK AT THESE PICTURES.

?

FIRST ONE SHOWS THE BACK DOOR OF THE SHIKISHIMA HOUSE...

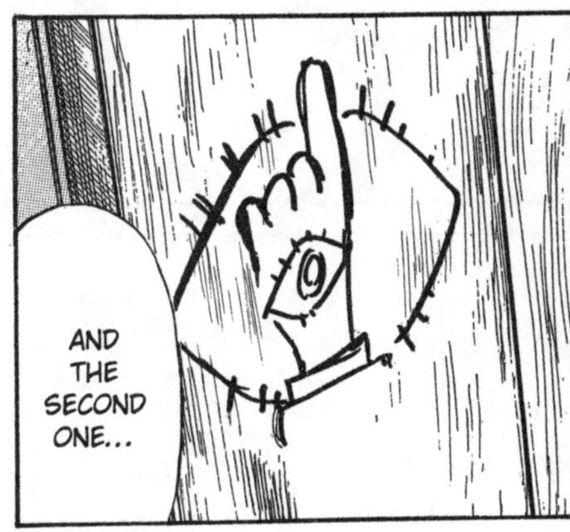
AND THE SECOND ONE...

...SHOWS THE T-SHIRTS WORN BY SHIKISHIMA'S RESEARCH GROUP STUDENTS.

WHAT'S THIS SYM-BOL?

YOU KNOW ABOUT THE FRIENDS?

HUH?
THIS IS THE EMBLEM OF PEOPLE WHO'RE FLOCKING AROUND SOME-ONE WHO CALLS HIMSELF THEIR FRIEND.

SO THEN WHO'S THIS "FRIEND"?
HE HEAD OF SOME RELIGIOUS CULT OR SOME-THING?

I DON'T KNOW... I'VE BEEN SNIFFING AROUND, BUT I CAN'T FIGURE OUT WHAT HIS GAME IS.
ONLY ...

WHILE I WAS INVESTIGATING SHIKISHIMA'S DISAPPEAR-ANCE...
...I HEARD HIS DAUGHTER HAD GOTTEN MIXED UP IN SOME WEIRD CULT.

AND THAT WEIRD CULT, I'M PRETTY SURE, IS THE FRIENDS.

HMM ...

WOULD YOU BELIEVE IT, THEY'RE HOLDING MEETINGS AT THE BUDOKAN. THEY'RE THAT BIG.
AND PEOPLE WHOSE CHILDREN HAVE GOTTEN MIXED UP WITH THEM ARE TRYING TO FORM A VICTIMS' GROUP TO GET THEM BACK.

YEAH? WHAT WAS THAT?

AND I HEARD SOMETHING VERY INTERESTING.

HUH... I HAD NO IDEA.
THESE DAYS, GROUPS LIKE THESE GROW HUGE BEFORE YOU'VE EVEN HEARD OF THEM.

...SO I ASKED THIS EXPERT ON RELIGIOUS CULTS ABOUT THE FRIENDS.
UH-HUH...

ACCORDING TO THIS EXPERT...
THE FRIENDS?

HMMM, ARE THEY A RELIGIOUS CULT OR NOT...
IT'S HARD TO SAY... USING THE CRITERIA I USE IN MY RESEARCH, THEY SORT OF ARE AND SORT OF AREN'T...

ONE THING, THOUGH...
THIS IS SOMETHING I JUST HAPPENED TO HEAR.

THERE'S A RUMOR THAT THE FRIENDS HAD SOME DISPUTE WITH THE PIERRE SPIRITUAL SOCIETY.
OF COURSE THIS IS JUST HEARSAY, YOU UNDERSTAND.

Pierre Ichimon of the Pierre Spiritual Society.
Slain in front of Tokyo Dome, where 100,000 believers
THE CULT HEADED BY PIERRE ICHIMONJI, WHO WAS STABBED TO DEATH THE OTHER DAY.

THE PIERRE SPIRITUAL SOCIETY? YOU MEAN...

YUP...

SO THEN, I WENT STRAIGHT OVER TO THE PIERRE SPIRITUAL SOCIETY HEAD-QUARTERS.

ACTUALLY... I'M HERE ON A DIFFERENT CASE!!
THE GROUP REPRE-SENTED BY THIS SYMBOL. DID PIERRE...

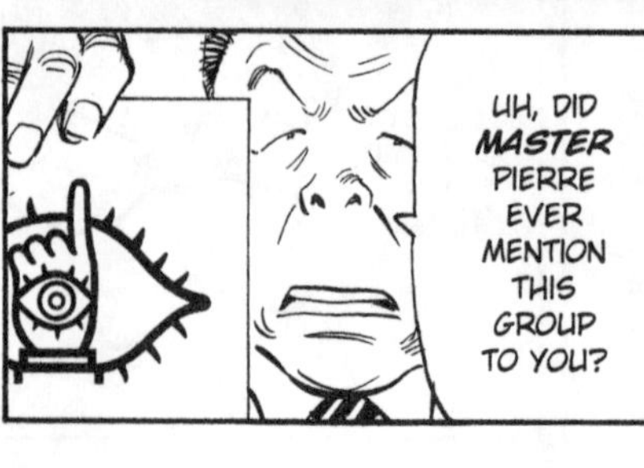
UH, DID *MASTER* PIERRE EVER MENTION THIS GROUP TO YOU?

ACCORD-ING TO THE GUY THERE...
WE'VE ALREADY TOLD THE POLICE EVERY-THING WE KNOW, ALL RIGHT?!
JUST HURRY UP AND ARREST THE MURDER-ER!!

OH...

THIS...
YES, HE SAID HE KNEW THE MAN WHO LEADS THE GROUP.

WHAT?
HE KNEW THIS "FRIEND"?

MASTER SAID THE GUY WAS HOPE-LESS...

HE WAS A COLLEGE STUDENT, I THINK. HE AIMED TOO LOW AND HAD NO GUTS... MASTER SAID.

BUT HOW DID HE KNOW HIM?

ABOUT 17 YEARS AGO...
...THEY UNDERWENT SPIRITUAL TRAINING TOGETHER IN A CERTAIN SECT...

IN THE SAME SECT?

HOWEVER, MASTER PIERRE REVEALED LATER THAT THAT WAS NOT THE SORT OF SPIRITUAL TRAINING HE HAD BEEN SEEKING.
MASTER PIERRE THEN WAS ENLIGHTENED, THROUGH HIS OWN SPIRITUAL POWERS, TO TEACHINGS THAT HAD NEVER BEFORE--

WHAT WAS HIS NAME?
DID MASTER PIERRE TELL YOU THE MAN'S NAME?

*Spiritual Training Join Now

*Hot Bento Lunches

I'D FINALLY TRACED THIS "FRIEND" TO THE ELEMENTARY SCHOOL HE'D ATTENDED.

I WENT THROUGH THEIR GRADUATION ALBUMS, LOOKING AT EVERY SINGLE NAME AND COMPARING THEM TO THE SCHOOL'S REGISTERS OF GRADUATES.

IF HE WAS A COLLEGE STUDENT 17 YEARS AGO, HE'D BE IN HIS MID-THIRTIES NOW...

HE WAS THERE. IT WAS THE "FRIEND" AS A SIXTH-GRADER...

HM?

ENDO KENJI?
THIS ADDRESS ...

FLAP

SURE ENOUGH. SAME ADDRESS!!

THAT CONVENIENCE STORE OWNER I INTERVIEWED IN THE NEIGHBOR-HOOD FOR THE SHIKISHIMA CASE...
COME TO US ANYTIME! WE'RE "KING MART, WHERE THE CUSTOMER IS ALWAYS KING"!!

...WAS IN THE SAME CLASS AS THIS "FRIEND"!!

Chapter 4 Yama-san

YOUR RICE-BALLS ARE ALL MIXED UP!! KOMBU GOES ON THE LEFT!! SALMON GOES IN THE MIDDLE!!

UH... YES-SIR!!

Chapter 4
Yama-san

...

BUT THE POOR GUY WAS GETTING RAKED OVER THE COALS BY HIS FRANCHISE SUPERVISOR.

WHAT IS OUR CATCH-PHRASE HERE AT KING MART, MR. ENDO?!

IT'S, UH... "KING MART, WHERE THE CUSTOMER IS ALWAYS KING"!!

SO, YOU DIDN'T GET TO INTERVIEW THIS ENDO KENJI THAT TIME...
AND YOUR INVESTIGA-TION INTO THIS "FRIEND" STOPPED THERE?

NO ...
?

SINCE I WAS AROUND THERE ANYWAY, I DECIDED TO VISIT THEIR TEACHER.

UH-HUH.
AND?

HE TOLD ME SOME-THING KINDA ODD.
KIND OF ODD?

TRRR

EXCUSE ME.
BIP

YEAH, HELLO ...
OH... HIRO-YUKI ...

NO...I'M ALMOST DONE WITH WORK TODAY... UH-HUH...
I WAS THINKING OF GOING OVER THERE SOON.

I'LL GIVE YOU A BUZZ WHEN I GET CLOSE BY, SO COULD YOU COME OUT?
I'VE GOT SOME-THING I WANT TO GIVE YOU.

DON'T BE LIKE THAT, CHO-SAN. COME INSIDE AND STAY AWHILE.

SHOHEI'S LOOKING FORWARD TO SEEING HIS GRAMPY.
UH... WELL, I'LL JUST GIVE YOU A CALL LATER, ALL RIGHT? BYE, THEN...

UH... CHO-SAN ...
BIP

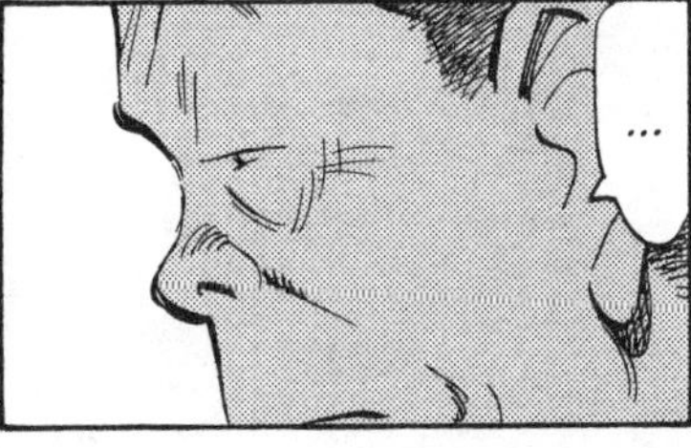
...

MY GRAND-SON'S BIRTHDAY TODAY...

A-HA, SO THAT PIKACHU IN YOUR BAG'S A PRESENT FOR THE BOY, CHO-SAN?

UH... YEAH.
TOY
CERATOPS

SO GRANDPA'S OFF TO A BIRTHDAY PARTY! HEADING OFF TO YOUR DAUGHTER'S HOME AFTER THIS?
WELL ...

IT DOESN'T QUITE WORK LIKE THAT...
WHY NOT?

MY DAUGHTER YUMIKO AND I...
WE DON'T GET ALONG ALL THAT WELL...

WHAT'S THE MATTER?
THIS ISN'T LIKE YOU, CHO-SAN.

WELL... THIS IS ONE CASE ...
...I'M HAVING A HARD TIME SOLVING ...

DID SOMETHING HAPPEN? TO STRAIN RELATIONS BETWEEN YOU?

SOME-THING? WELL...

YOU KNOW TRACK AND FIELD DAY AT SCHOOL?
UH-HUH ...

SHE WAS GOING TO RUN IN A RELAY. I PROMISED HER I'D BE THERE TO WATCH...

BUT I GOT THERE TWO HOURS LATE. THE WHOLE THING WAS OVER.

WELL, THAT HAPPENS WHEN YOU'RE ON A CASE.

HER WEDDING? I WAS THREE HOURS LATE FOR THAT.
...

NOT ONLY WASN'T I THERE TO WALK HER DOWN THE AISLE...
...I MISSED THE WHOLE DAMN RECEPTION. SHE WAS CHANGING OUT OF HER WEDDING DRESS WHEN I GOT THERE.

...

AND WHEN I GOT THE PHONE CALL SAYING MY WIFE WAS DYING...

I GOT TO THE HOSPITAL FOUR HOURS LATER.

YUMIKO HASN'T SPOKEN A WORD TO ME SINCE...

YAMA-SAN, I'M RETIRING IN A WEEK.

THIS IS NO TIME TO BE TALKING ABOUT WORK, CHO-SAN...

CHO-SAN ...

LET'S GET BACK TO THIS "FRIEND."

YOU'RE LOOKING AT A HOPELESS IDIOT WHO'S SPENT HIS WHOLE DAMN LIFE THINKING WORK WAS ALL THAT MATTERED.
AND THAT IDIOT IS TELLING YOU NOW, WITH THE GUT FEELING THAT COMES FROM A LIFE-TIME AT THIS...

...

...THAT THIS CASE IS GOING TO TURN INTO SOMETHING SERIOUSLY SCARY. IN FACT, IT MAY ALREADY HAVE!!
AND THAT'S WHY I WANT YOU TO TAKE IT OVER FROM ME!!

THE TEACHER IN CHARGE OF THIS "FRIEND" AND KENJI'S CLASS THOUGHT BACK...

* The Class of '71 graduated in March of 1972.

...WAS COMPLETELY BENT OUT OF SHAPE ...

HELLO
...

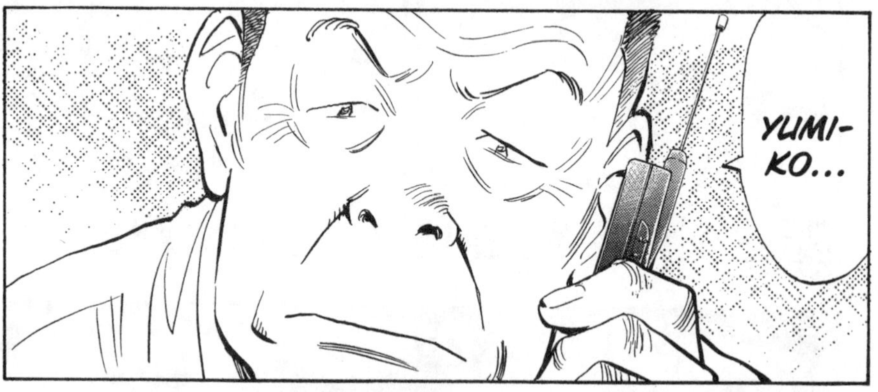
YUMI-
KO...

FATHER
...
...

WE'RE ABOUT TO START WITH SHOHEI'S BIRTHDAY PARTY, SO...

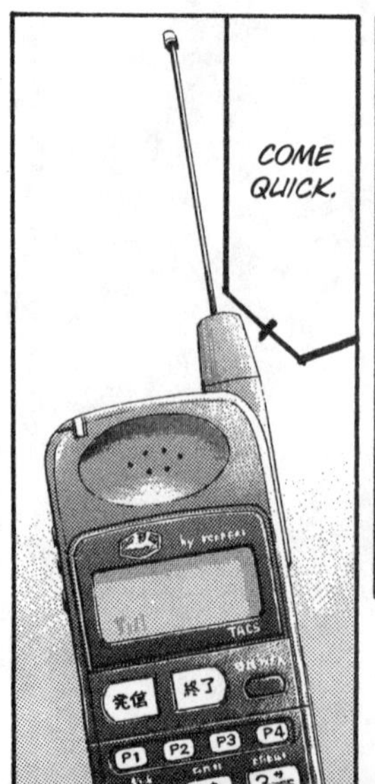
COME QUICK.
発信
終了
P1
P2
P3
P4

IS IT... REALLY ALL RIGHT, YUMIKO ...?

...

IF YOU'RE NO MORE THAN AN HOUR LATE, I'LL FORGIVE YOU. SO JUST COME QUICK.

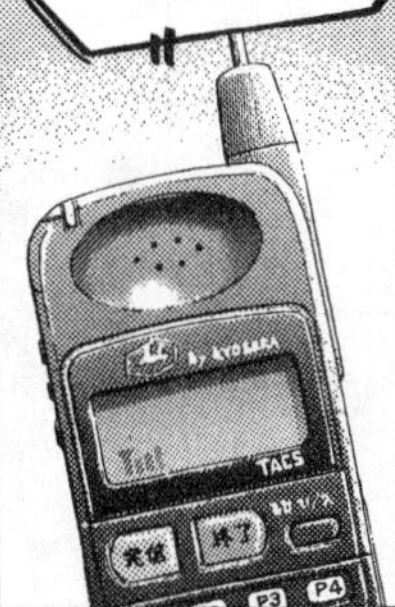

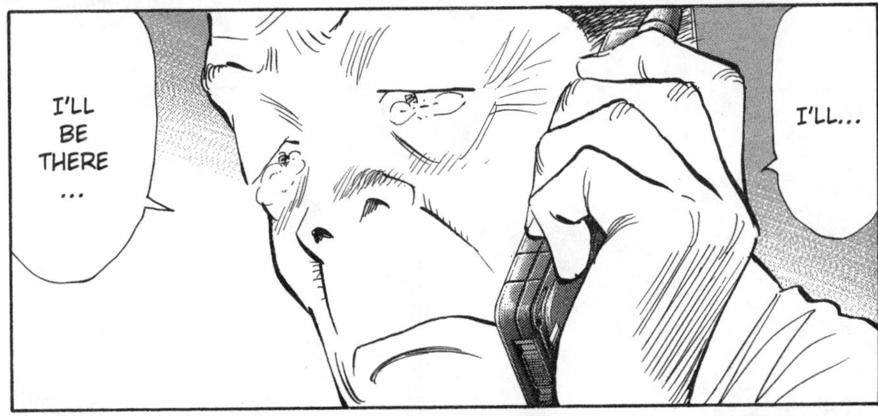
I'LL...
I'LL BE THERE ...

BIP

YAMA-SAN ...

WHAT'RE YOU SITTING THERE FOR?

THIS CASE IS MINE NOW, ALL RIGHT? YOU JUST LEAVE IT TO ME...

YAMA-SAN...

...AND GET YOURSELF OVER TO YOUR GRANDSON'S BIRTHDAY PARTY. C'MON, GIT.

THANKS, YAMA-SAN...
WHAT'RE YOU TALKING ABOUT, CHO-SAN? THAT'S WHAT I'M HERE FOR.

WONDER... HOW IT'LL WORK OUT...

TUMP
OH, COME ON! IT'LL WORK OUT JUST FINE!!

*Police Station

*Locker Room

...OF REJECTING HIM.

THUNK

TOY

FWAP

DETECTIVE FOUND DEAD

Severe external hemorrhaging Just one week before retirement.

I HATED SHOJO MANGA, SO ALL I READ WERE BOYS' COMICS.

*Shonen Sunday and Weekly Shonen Magazine

THOSE DREAMY GUYS WHO SHOWED UP IN SHOJO MANGA DIDN'T EXIST IN REAL LIFE.

NOBODY EVER REALLY GOT SAVED BY A HAND-SOME PRINCE ON A WHITE HORSE.

BUT THAT TIME ...

...I THOUGHT MAYBE KNIGHTS IN SHINING ARMOR REALLY DID EXIST, AFTER ALL...
Chapter 5
Humanity's Final Hour

KING mart
UMMM, EXCUSE ME!!

UH... YES, MA'AM!!

THIS COPIER HERE DOESN'T DO POST-CARDS?!

UH... SORRY, NO.
OUR MACHINE CAN'T DO POST-CARDS...

HEY...

SHEESH, YUKIJI. IT'S YOU!!
I WOULDN'T GO AROUND SAYING "SHEESH" TO A CUSTOMER. YOU WANT THAT FRANCHISE COP ON YOUR CASE?

HERE!! *YOU* TAKE CARE OF THIS, KENJI!!

HUH? WHAT THE HELL'S THIS...
Invitation to Class of '71 Reunion
How are you, everybody? Last year was the 25th anniversary of our graduation from elementary school, but we missed the occasion. So... let's have our 25th year reunion one year late!
If you are in touch with anybody from the Class of '71, please let them know.

INVITATION FOR OUR CLASS REUNION. THIS IS THE ORIGINAL.
CLASS REUNION?

GRADE SIX, CLASS THREE!
ELEMENTARY SCHOOL REUNION!!

OH...

I'LL TELL YOU THIS-- *I* SURE AS HELL DON'T WANT TO BE IN CHARGE OF THIS THING.

I HATE THESE THINGS.
I MEAN, WHO WANTS TO GET IN TOUCH AFTER ALL THESE YEARS?

ALL YOU DO IS SIT AROUND GETTING DRUNK AND SAYING "GOSH, YOU HAVEN'T CHANGED A BIT"!!
AND EVERY-BODY'S ASKING IF YOU GOT MARRIED AND IF YOU HAVE ANY KIDS--LIKE IT'S ANY OF THEIR GODDAMN BUSINESS!!

SO, NO LUCK IN THAT DEPART-MENT AFTER ALL?
WHAD-DAYA MEAN, "AFTER ALL"?!

UH... NOTHING, REALLY ...

SO OKAY, I'M NOT MARRIED. I DON'T HAVE ANY KIDS. SO WHAT?
I MEAN, LOOK AT YOURSELF. YOU'RE JUST TAKING CARE OF YOUR SISTER'S KID, RIGHT?

BASICALLY, YOU SEE EACH OTHER AGAIN AFTER ALL THESE YEARS, AND YOU'RE LIKE, WHAT A *LETDOWN,* I SHOULD NEVER HAVE COME!

?

PHLAP
HERE!! THIS IS THE LIST WITH ALL THE NAMES AND ADDRESSES.

OTCHO, OF COURSE, ISN'T ON THERE.

YOU WANT *ME* TO SEND THEM OUT?
THE HARD PART WAS LOOKING EVERYBODY UP, OKAY?! THESE ARE ALL THE PEOPLE I COULD FIND CURRENT ADDRESSES FOR.

LOOK, *THAT'S* WHAT WE'RE HOLDING THIS REUNION FOR, ALL RIGHT?!
THIS ISN'T ABOUT GETTING WASTED AND TALKING ABOUT THE GOOD OLD DAYS!!

WE'RE GOING TO GATHER AS MUCH INFORMATION ON OTCHO AS WE CAN, GOT IT?!

YOU REALLY CAN'T FIND OUT...
...WHERE OTCHO IS?

NOPE. THE MAN WHO INVENTED THIS SYMBOL AS A KID HAS GONE TOTALLY MISSING...

...WHILE SOME GUY CALLING HIMSELF A "FRIEND" HAS FORMED A MYSTERY GROUP WITH THIS SYMBOL AS ITS EMBLEM.
HE'S ATTRACTING THOUSANDS OF MEMBERS AND STARTING TO DO SOMETHING CRAZY.

MEAN-WHILE, DONKEY HAS COMMITTED SUICIDE...

WHAT DO ***YOU*** THINK OF ALL THIS?

...

I'LL TELL YOU SOMETHING ELSE THAT'S INTEREST-ING.

Japanese trading company man goes missing in Thailand.
Met with road accident in jungle?
NINE YEARS AGO, WHEN HE WAS WORKING FOR A TRADING CORPORATION, OTCHO HAD AN ACCIDENT IN THAILAND AND WENT MISSING FOR A WEEK.

HE QUIT THE COMPANY RIGHT AFTER *THAT.*
WELL, I WANTED TO KNOW WHERE HE WENT AFTER THAT, SO I ASKED AROUND.

AND?

A GUY AT A RIVAL TRADING COMPANY, WHO WAS IN THAILAND AT THE SAME TIME AS OTCHO AND KNEW HIM PRETTY WELL, TOLD ME HE SAW HIM EIGHT YEARS AGO.
WHERE?

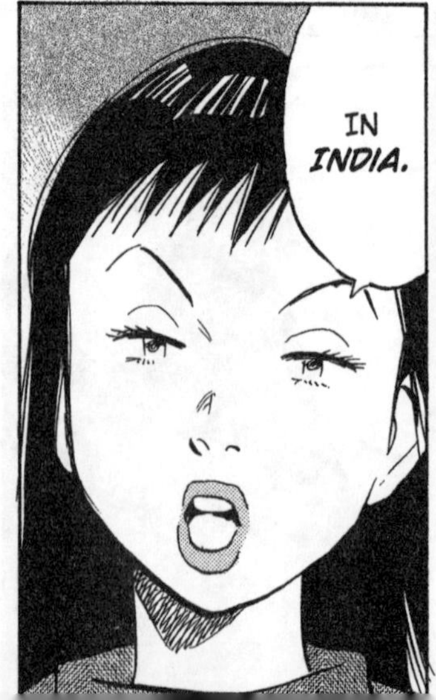
IN *INDIA.*

INDIA?

ACCORD-
ING TO
THE
GUY...

YOU CAN
BET I WAS
PRETTY
SUR-
PRISED.

IN FACT,
WHEN I
FIRST
SAW
HIM, I
DOUBTED
MY OWN
EYES.
I DIDN'T
REALLY THINK
IT COULD BE
HIM, BUT I
SAID HELLO
JUST IN
CASE AND
SURE
ENOUGH
IT WAS...

YOU
WOULDN'T
BELIEVE
WHAT HE
LOOKED
LIKE...
...OH,
AND
HE
SAID...

I'M GOING TO TIBET.

OTCHO
...

WHY DIDN'T YOU COME?

HUH?
TO THE VICTIMS' GROUP MEETING THE OTHER DAY. WHY DIDN'T YOU COME?

UH... WELL
...

YOU *WOULD'VE* COME, BACK THEN...
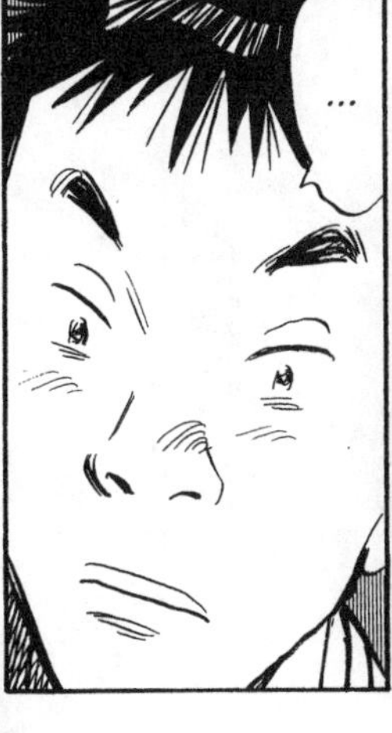
...

FORGET IT... SO SEND OUT THOSE REUNION INVITATIONS, OKAY?
HEY
...

UM...
I...

DON'T!!

I, UH ...

MAKING EX-CUSES ...
...IS SOME-THING A KNIGHT IN SHINING ARMOR NEVER, EVER DOES!!

I...UM... GOTTA MAKE SOMETHING OF THIS BUSINESS...
YOU KNOW, GOTTA FEED MY MOM AND THIS BABY AND EVERYTHING...

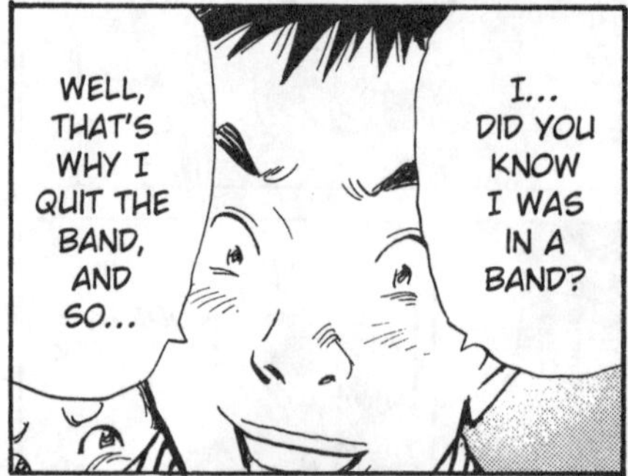
I... DID YOU KNOW I WAS IN A BAND?
WELL, THAT'S WHY I QUIT THE BAND, AND SO...

I KNEW I SHOULDN'T HAVE COME...
EH?

NOTHIN'. SEE YA.

HEY... YUKIJI ...

WHEN YOU QUIT YOUR BAND...

?

WAS THAT THE ***REAL*** REASON YOU QUIT?

BAM

WAS THAT THE REAL REASON ...
...I QUIT?

WHY...
...DID I QUIT THE BAND, AGAIN?

OUR FRIEND!

A LOT OF RELIGIOUS LEADERS ARE BEING "REJECTED" BY THE COSMOS RECENTLY...

WHAT IS THE COSMOS TRYING TO LEAD YOU TO DO THROUGH THIS, OUR FRIEND?

WHAT DO YOU THINK IT'S TRYING TO MAKE ME DO?

OOOH
HERE!! I BELIEVE THE AIM IS RELIGIOUS UNIFICATION.

BUB
THAT'S BRIL-LIANT!
THAT WAY, THE WHOLE WORLD WILL BECOME FRIENDS.
HUB
WHAT A BRILLIANT PLAN!

THAT ISN'T IT, ACTUALLY ...

HUBBA
HUH?

THE COSMOS IS TELLING ME TO MAKE MY DREAM A REALITY.

MAKE YOUR DREAM A REALITY?
WHAT IS YOUR DREAM, OUR FRIEND?

MY DREAM ...
A DREAM IS SOME-THING THAT CAN ONLY BE MADE REAL BY THOSE WHO CONTINUE TO KEEP ALIVE ITS INITIAL IMPULSE.

ITS INITIAL IMPULSE ...
SO YOU'VE HELD ONTO THIS DREAM FOR A LONG TIME, OUR FRIEND?

PLEASE LET US HEAR WHAT THAT DREAM IS...

WORLD DOMINATION, MY FRIENDS.

ZWOON

ZWOON

ZWOON

ZWOON
IN DECEMBER 2000, HUMANITY WILL MEET ITS FINAL HOUR.

Chapter 6 Kamisama

URRGH... URRGH...

WAAGH, WAAGH, WAAGH!!

WUGH WUGH WUGH WUGH WUGH WUGH!!

WAAAAAAA-AAAAAGH!!

WHAT'S THE MATTER?

YOU WERE SCREAMING IN YOUR SLEEP AGAIN.

DON'T WORRY ABOUT IT. JUST DON'T WORRY ABOUT IT.

HAWAII

Chapter 6
Kamisama

DON'T WORRY ABOUT IT? 'COURSE WE'RE GONNA WORRY ABOUT IT.
KAMISAMA DREAMS SOMETHING, YOU KNOW IT'S GONNA HAPPEN.

I MEAN, RIGHT AFTER HE TOLD TOKU-SAN THIS WOULD BE THE YEAR HE HITS IT BIG...
OL' TOKU-SAN GOT HIT BY A TRUCK. WE OUGHTA VISIT HIM IN THE HOSPITAL, I THINK HE'S ABOUT TO DIE.

WHAT DID YOU DREAM THIS TIME, KAMISAMA?
STOP CALLING ME THAT!! I'M NOT A GOD!!

AND DON'T DO THAT!!

WE'LL BRING YOU YOUR BREAKFAST IN A MINUTE, KAMISAMA.
IT WAS RAINING REAL HARD, THOUGH, SO IT'S PRETTY SLIM PICKINS...

YOU GUYS EAT IT.
I CAN RUSTLE UP MY OWN BREAK-FAST.
HAWAII

DON'T SAY THAT. HERE, EAT IT. PLEASE!
IF WE EAT YOUR SHARE, THE EVIL EYE WILL GET US.
I DON'T WANT ANY OFFERINGS!!

WE THOUGHT, WE GIVE YOU THIS, YOU COULD TELL US A STORY.
YEAH, YOU LEARN A LOT FROM HIS STORIES.

WHAT'S THE POINT OF LISTENING TO ME TALK?
PLEEEZE! TELL US A STORY!

YOU KNOW ALL I'VE GOT ARE BOWLING STORIES.
TELL US ONE, TELL US ONE!
KLAP KLAP KLAP KLAP

OH, ALL RIGHT. HERE GOES.
SO. A BOWLING LANE IS EXACTLY 1.06 METERS WIDE.
HAWAII

UH-HUH, YEAH.

EVERYONE BOWLS THE BALL AIMING FOR A STRIKE, RIGHT?

YEP, SURE DO.

HAWAII
SO WHEN YOU LET GO OF THE BALL, YOU'RE FOCUSED RIGHT IN THE MIDDLE.

HAWAII
BUT IF YOUR ANGLE'S OFF BY EVEN JUST A COUPLE DEGREES ...
...BY THE TIME THE BALL REACHES THE PINS, 18.28 METERS AWAY, IT'S WAY OFF TARGET.

DISTANCE FROM THE HEAD PIN TO THE GUTTER IS 53 CENTI-METERS.
THAT'S ALL THE DIFFERENCE THERE IS BETWEEN A STRIKE AND A GUTTER BALL.

HUH ...

SO?
SO, THAT'S THE STORY.

SEE YA.

SURE LEARN A LOT...
SURE DO...

OH... THAT'S RIGHT.

GOT SOME-THING TO TELL YOU, HAMA-SAN.
AWAII

HEH... ME?

WATCH OUT FOR KIDS TODAY.

KIDS?
?
WHAT'S THAT MEAN?

KING
たばこ
酒

HELLO! WELCOME TO--

NIKKEI AVERAGE DOWN BY 150 YEN, HM...
HO-HO, SO IT'S 98 AFTER 95, IS IT? GOTTA HAND IT TO THAT BILL GATES...

?
NEW YORK SHARE PRICES STILL RISING, UH-HUH...

KVOSH
...

WHAT... WAS THAT?
MAKE HIM LEAVE.

EASY FOR YOU TO SAY...

HE'S STARING AT THE LUNCHES. STARING AT 'EM!

?
HE'S CALLING YOU. WHAT'S HE WANT?

HA
UH...YES. WHAT CAN I...

THIS HAM-BURGER LUNCH RIGHT HERE...
YES?

IT'S PAST ITS SELL-BY DATE.

ULP...
VERY SORRY! I'LL REMOVE IT RIGHT AW--

KLAMP
HAWAII

WHAT'S OKAY? I SAID, I'LL REMOVE IT!!
NO, REALLY. IT'S OKAY.

WH-WHAT?

IT'S OKAY.

WHAT... WHAT IS IT?

NO IT'S NOT OKAY !!
UH-OH?

WOW, YOU'RE IN FOR A REAL HARD TIME.
WAII
HUH?

HAWAI

THIS LITTLE BOY, ON THE OTHER HAND...
HAW

SHE'S NOT A BOY, SHE'S A GIRL!!
BABOOOO!!

HEY... WHAT IS IT, KANNA?!!
HAWAII
BABOO, BABOO!!

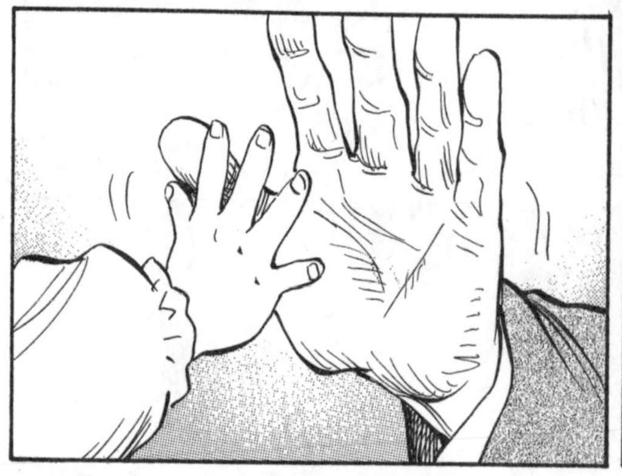

...IS REALLY SOMETHING.

DAA... DA!!

?
WELL, THEN.

HEY... THAT LUNCH!!
YOU'RE TOSSING IT ANYWAY, RIGHT?

WHAT ON EARTH?
...

DAA... DA!!
?

THAT DREAM WAS A REAL DOOZY THIS TIME...

A REAL DOOZY, DID YOU SAY, KAMISAMA?
I'M NOT A GOD, OKAY? STOP CALLING ME THAT.

STILL, DON'T ASK ME WHY, BUT I JUST KNOW IT...
SOME-THING REALLY HAIRY'S GOING TO HAPPEN...

HUH...

WE'LL BE FINE, THOUGH.
AFTER ALL, NO MATTER WHAT HAPPENS...
HAWAII

...*OUR* LIFE ISN'T GOING TO CHANGE MUCH...

HELP... HELP!!

NGH?
IT'S ALREADY STARTED? THAT'S SOONER THAN I THOUGHT...

BUNCH OF KIDS... HAMA-SAN... AT THE PARK!!
OHHHH, *THAT*...

THWOK
FRIGGIN' TROLL!!
YOU'RE DISGUSTING, YOU STINKIN' HOBO!!
WHAK

THWOK
THUNK
UNGH !!
UNGH !!

LOOK AT HIM, ROLLIN' IN THE DIRT! OINK, OINK!!
LET'S THROW 'IM IN THE RIVER!!

WHAP
THWOK
URRGH ...

THAT'S ENOUGH, BOYS.

HAWAII

WHAT'D YOU SAY?! HUH?!
YOU WANNA GET THROWN IN THE RIVER TOO?!

WATCH IT! THERE'S A TURD RIGHT THERE IN FRONT OF YOU!!
HYARGH !!

SOMEWHERE IN THE DARK THERE. IT'S STILL STEAMING-- I JUST LAID IT.
YOU WOULDN'T WANT TO STEP IN THAT.
HAWAI

YAAAARGH!!

WHICH ONE OF YOU'S FUMIYA?
HAWAII
HEH?

YOU FUMIYA?
H-HOW'D YOU KNOW THAT?

ATE OUT AGAIN TODAY, HUH? BURGERS.
THAT'S ALL YOU'VE EVER EATEN FOR DINNER SINCE GRADE SCHOOL. YOUR MOMMA'S WAITING FOR YOU WITH A WARM, HOME-COOKED MEAL.

HOW... IN HELL'D YOU KNOW THAT?!

I DON'T KNOW *HOW* I KNOW IT, I JUST KNOW IT.
WHICH ONE OF YOU'S KOICHI?

HEH?

STEALING MONEY FROM YOUR FOLKS AND SPENDING IT ALL IN GAME CENTERS.
YOU KNOW WHAT THEY'RE WORKING SO HARD TO SAVE THAT MONEY FOR? YOUR EDUCATION!!

HOW... THE HELL D'YOU KNOW STUFF LIKE THAT?!
LIKE I TOLD YOU, I JUST KNOW IT, ALL RIGHT?!

URRGH... KAMI-SAMA...

KAMI... SAMA? LIKE, "GOD"?

BELIEVE ME, I'M NO GOD.

...

LISTEN. IN BOWLING, IF YOU HURL THE BALL STRAIGHT DOWN THE MIDDLE...
REAL HARD, BECAUSE YOU'RE AIMING FOR A STRIKE...

...YOU GET STUCK WITH THE BIG TWO. THAT'S A SPLIT LEAVING THE TWO OUTSIDE PINS.
YOU ALMOST NEVER PICK UP A SPARE AFTER THAT.

?

SO DON'T WORRY ABOUT BOWLING THE BALL DEAD CENTER. BEING SLIGHTLY OFF TO THE SIDE IS JUST FINE.
YOU GET WHAT I'M SAYING?

HE'S... CREEPIN' ME OUT.
MAN, WHAT'S HE TALKIN' ABOUT ANYWAY?

IF YOU DON'T GET IT, YOU WANT TO HEAR MORE? WHEN ONLY ONE OF THE TEN PINS IS LEFT STANDING...
UH... NO THANKS!!
LET'S GET THE HELL OUTTA HERE, DUDES!!

YOU WERE RIGHT... AGAIN... KAMI-SAMA...

YOU TOLD ME TO WATCH OUT FOR KIDS TODAY...

LET'S GO GET SOME SLEEP, HAMA-SAN. TOMORROW'S GONNA BE MORE OR LESS OKAY.
REALLY?
WELL, TOMORROW ANYWAY...

...THAT A HUGE MONSTER'S GOING TO APPEAR...

ZWOOON
PSHOO
PSHOO
PSHOO
ZWOOOON
...IN DECEMBER 2000. AND HUMANITY WILL MEET ITS FINAL HOUR.

Chapter 7 Kiriko's Desk Drawer

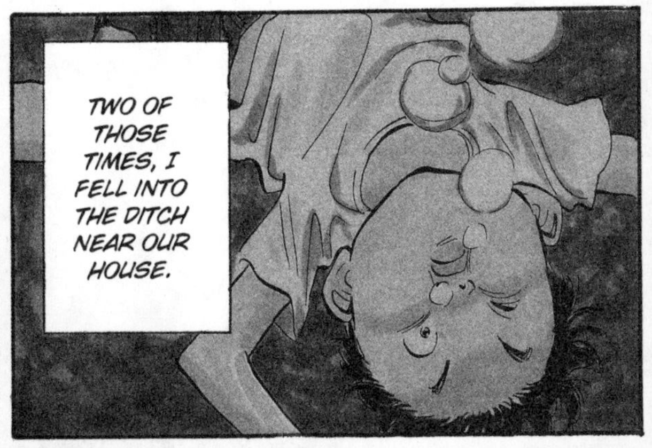

PLISH

PLASH

THE ONE WHO DID SAVE THE LIFE OF THIS FUTURE HERO, DESTINED TO DEFEND THE EARTH IN ITS HOUR OF CRISIS, WAS HIS SISTER. THAT IS, MY SISTER.

Chapter 7
Kiriko's Desk Drawer

NOBODY DIES IN SHALLOW WATER LIKE THAT.

20世紀少年
Twentieth Century Boys

HULL-LOW, WALL-COME...
酒
Erika Yamada
*Liquor

I'VE FIGURED OUT WHY YOUR SALES DON'T GO UP, MR. ENDO.
FANK-YOOO.

UH...SORRY. I KNOW ERIKA, OUR PART-TIMER, ISN'T VERY BRIGHT AND CHEERY...
NO, I MEAN THIS. THIS THING!!

WHAT... THING...?

WHOEVER SAW A CONVENIENCE STORE OWNER WITH A BABY ON HIS BACK?
UH... YEAH, BUT SHE'S ...

YOU EXPECT CUSTOMERS TO ENJOY SHOPPING IN A STORE WITH SOMETHING LIKE THAT AROUND ALL THE TIME?

SOME-THING... LIKE THAT?
BUT SHE'S ...

YOUR SISTER'S CHILD, I BELIEVE.
UH... YES.

YOUR SISTER IS MISSING SO YOU AND YOUR MOTHER ARE LOOKING AFTER HER CHILD.
UH... THAT'S RIGHT.

WHAT DO YOU INTEND TO DO ABOUT THIS?
IN-TEND... TO DO...?

YES, INTEND TO DO. HOW ABOUT MAKING A DECISION ABOUT THIS TODAY?!
DECI-SION... ABOUT WHAT?

...

EITHER YOU SEND THAT CHILD TO DAYCARE...
...OR YOU CANCEL YOUR CONTRACT WITH US. ONE OR THE OTHER.

HULL-LOW... WALL-COME...

WHY CAN'T SHE SPEAK PROPERLY, THAT GIRL?!

WELL ANYWAY, IF THAT'S WHAT HE SAYS, I DON'T THINK WE HAVE A CHOICE.

...

THOUGH WE CAN BARELY AFFORD TO PAY THAT NO-GOOD PART-TIMER'S WAGES. HOW WE'LL COME UP WITH THE MONEY FOR DAYCARE I REALLY DON'T KNOW...

GOD KNOWS WE HAVE ENOUGH TROU-BLES.
IT COSTS A PRETTY PENNY, DOESN'T IT, DAY-CARE...

WELL, WHAT CHOICE DO WE HAVE?
STAYING OPEN ALL NIGHT ***AND*** TAKING CARE OF KANNA, ONE OF US WILL END UP COLLAPSING.

THAT KIRIKO, FOR CRYING OUT LOUD...
LEAVING US WITH THIS BABY OF HERS... AND NOT A WORD ABOUT WHO FATHERED HER...

I'M DONE, MA...

THIS IS WHY I WAS AGAINST THE WHOLE IDEA. I ***TOLD*** YOU NOT TO TURN THE PLACE INTO A KING MART.
ALWAYS HAVE THEM COMING AROUND, TELLING YOU WHAT TO DO. THEN THEY TAKE ALL YOUR MONEY.

WE SHOULD'VE JUST STAYED A LIQUOR STORE.
THIS IS WHAT WE GET FOR CLOSING DOWN YOUR FATHER'S FAMILY BUSINESS.

NOT ONE GOOD THING, SINCE WE JOINED THAT FRANCHISE. NOT ONE.

SIS...

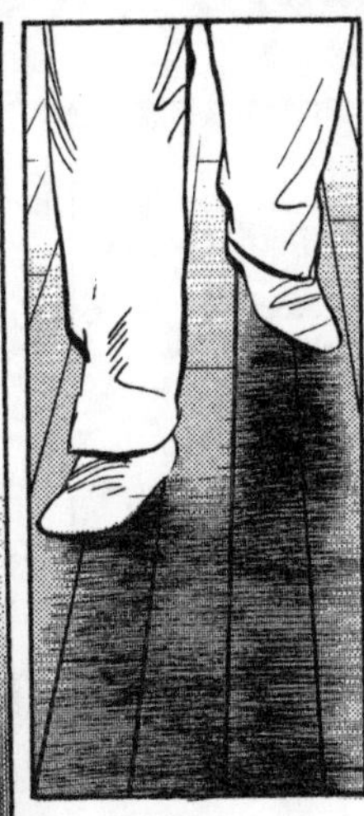

KREE

*Endo Liquors

WAGH! WAGH!
STOP CRYING. HURRY UP AND TAKE OFF YOUR SHIRT!!

WHY'D YOU HAVE TO FALL IN AGAIN?
YOUR UNDER-PANTS TOO, COME ON!!

WAGH! WAGH!
IT'S CUZ YOU WERE LOOKING IN THE WATER AT SOME-THING, SIS.

I WANTED TO SEE WHAT IT WAS, SO I LOOKED OVER THE SIDE AND I FELL IN.

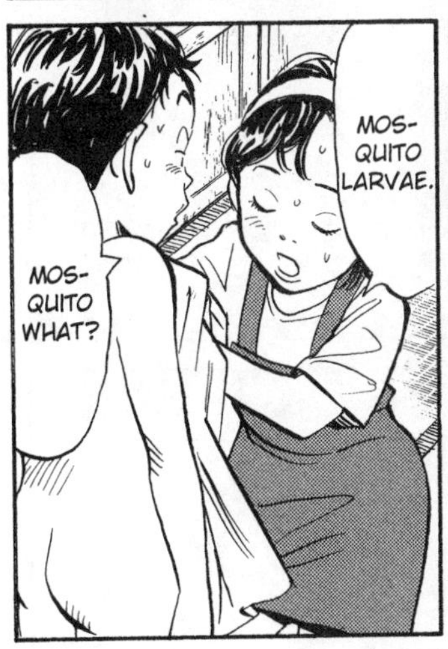
MOS-QUITO LARVAE.
MOS-QUITO WHAT?

BABIES. THEY'RE SO CUTE, THE WAY THEY WRIGGLE AROUND.

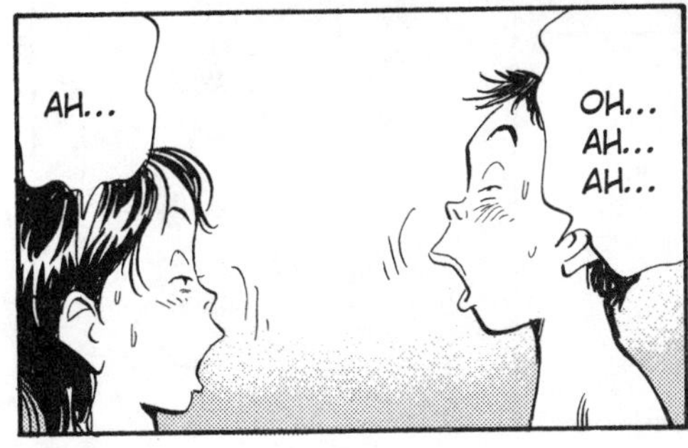
OH... AH... AH...
AH...

MY SISTER WAS SOAKING WET HER-SELF. SHE SPENT THE NEXT WEEK IN BED WITH A COLD...
SNIFFLE

AAH-CHOOO!!

VRUT
VRUT
HONDA

VRUT
VRUT
VRUT

HEY ...
STUPID.

WHAT WERE YOU DOING?

UH... WELL, I WAS ON MY MOTOR-BIKE AND...
I KNOW, I CAN SEE FOR MYSELF. THE DOCTOR SAID YOU'RE LUCKY TO BE ALIVE.

WHAT ABOUT... MA AND PA?

WENT HOME, SAYING THEY DON'T NEED THIS FOOL FOR A SON.

FIG-URES ...

GWEERR

I CAN'T BELIEVE YOU'RE HUNGRY.

WELL... I *AM* STILL ALIVE ...

I BOUGHT YOU SOME APPLES.

Tajiro Kawabata

ON THAT SAME DAY, THE UNIVERSITY MY SISTER WANTED TO GET INTO WAS HOLDING ITS ENTRANCE EXAMS. BUT I DIDN'T KNOW THAT UNTIL WAY LATER...
Microbiology Today
A Survey of the Latest Research
Tajiro Kawabata
Teito Publishing
Microbiology Today

MAYBE WHAT YOUR MAMA REALLY WANTED TO DO WAS GO TO COLLEGE TO STUDY MOSQUITO LARVAE OR SOMETHING...

THAT'S RIGHT, HER LETTERS WERE IN HERE...
KTUNK

LOOK AT THESE. THIS GUY WORKED FOR A REAL BLUE-CHIP COMPANY.
I DIDN'T EVEN KNOW SHE WAS DATING ANYONE LIKE THIS...

READ THESE WHEN SHE DISAPPEARED, HOPING TO FIND SOME CLUE WHERE SHE WENT.

HE ASKED YOUR MAMA TO MARRY HIM.
BUT SHE ...
貴理子様、
あなたが僕のプロポーズを
断わられたこと
"DEAR KIRIKO, IT WAS A GREAT SHOCK TO ME TO HAVE YOU TURN DOWN MY PROPOSAL OF MARRIAGE."
"BUT I UNDER-STAND YOUR REASON VERY WELL."

"I CAN UNDERSTAND THAT, WITH YOUR FATHER GONE, YOU FEEL YOUR MOTHER NEEDS YOU THERE TO HELP HER RUN YOUR FAMILY'S BUSINESS..."
"SO PLEASE ACCEPT THESE LAST WORDS FROM ME, BEFORE I VANISH FROM YOUR LIFE."

"I WISH YOU EVERY HAPPI-NESS."
...IS WHAT IT SAYS.

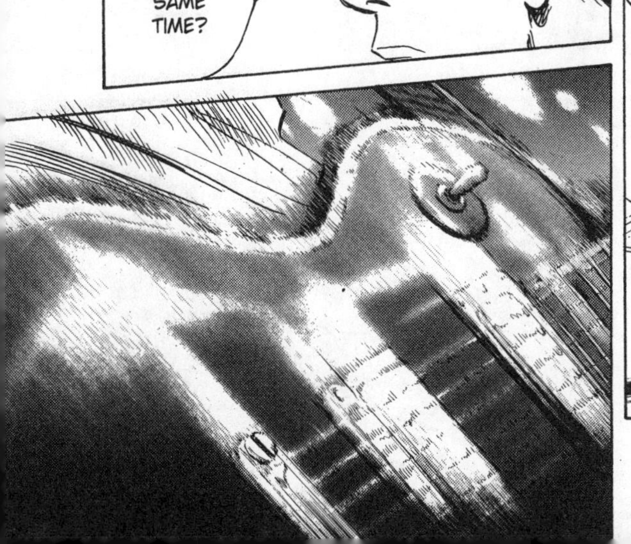
...AND WHAT WAS *I* DOING AROUND THAT SAME TIME?

SIS...

I ALWAYS DID WHAT-EVER THE HELL I WANTED...

...WHILE YOU ALWAYS ...

PLEASE TAKE THIS CHILD!!

PLEASE, PLEASE TAKE CARE OF KANNA FOR ME!!

I'M BEGGING YOU, PLEASE!!
THAT WAS THE ONE AND ONLY TIME, EVER, THAT MY SISTER ASKED FOR SOME-THING FOR HERSELF...

SO YOU SEE, KANNA ...
I GUESS THE GUY WHO WROTE THESE LETTERS IS NOT YOUR PAPA.

KTUNK
WHICH IS TOO BAD, SINCE HE'S PROBABLY PRETTY RICH...

?

THERE'S A LETTER STUCK IN THE BACK...

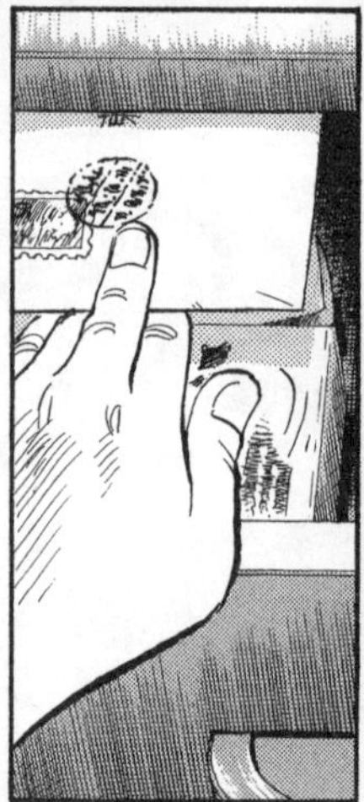

NO NAME OR RETURN ADDRESS ...

So your plan and my plan
turn out to be the same.
How marvelous, that I
was able to meet someone
with the same plan as mine.

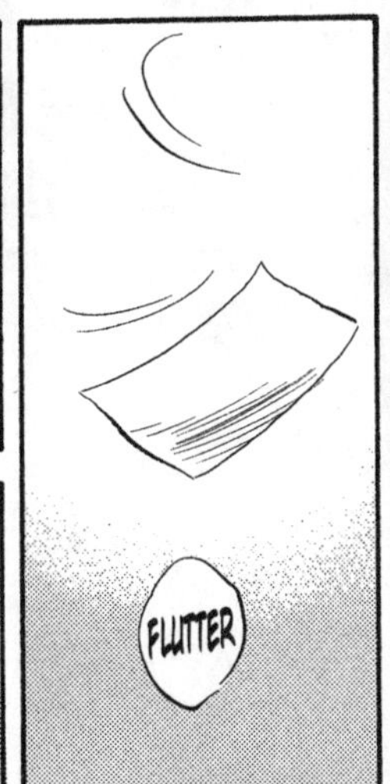

PHLAP

Chapter 8 Kiriko's Boyfriend

POK POK
遠藤家
*Endo Family
POK POK
POK POK
DINNNG

JUST LEAVE THE LIQUOR STORE TO ME, ALL RIGHT?

Chapter 8
Kiriko's Boyfriend

堂楽器店

¥26000

THE ELECTRIC GUITAR COST 26,000 YEN.

TO ME AT THE TIME, IN THE THIRD YEAR OF JUNIOR HIGH, IT WAS AN ASTRONOMICAL FIGURE.

*Instruments

HOW COME ...

WHY'S THIS IN A LETTER TO MY SISTER?

THIS SYMBOL ...

KEN-JIII!!
!!

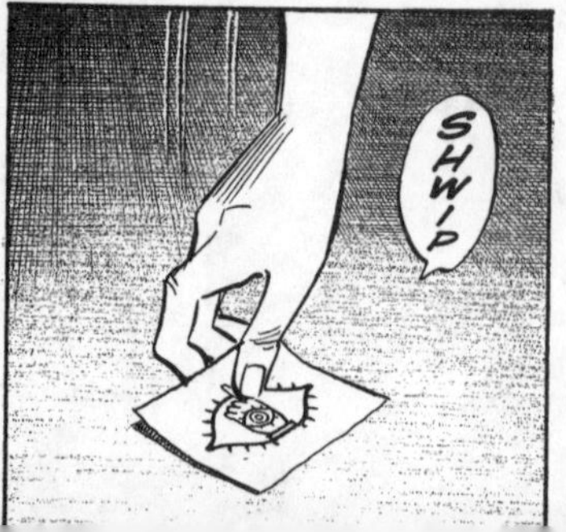
SHWIP

OH, SO *THIS* IS WHERE YOU WERE!!

UH... UH, YEAH... WHAT IS IT, MA?
KRUSH

HE'S BACK. THAT SALES FELLOW FROM HEAD-QUARTERS, OTAKE!!
OH ...

SAYS HE CAME TO TELL YOU THEY'LL TERMINATE OUR CONTRACT IF WE DON'T PUT KANNA IN DAYCARE!
OH ...

WHAT DO YOU PLAN TO DO? WE'VE STILL GOT PILES OF DEBT TO PAY OFF.

HEY, MA?

WHY'D SIS ALWAYS TAKE SUCH GOOD CARE OF ME ALL THE TIME?

WHAT.

WELL... THAT'S BECAUSE ...
UH... BEFORE YOU WERE... WELL, BORN, SEE...

BEFORE I WAS ***BORN?***

1959
YOU... YOU'RE JOKING, RIGHT ?!!

WISH I WAS...
THOUGHT IT MIGHT BE A BAD DREAM SO I TRIED WAKING UP, BUT LOOKS LIKE I ALREADY WAS AWAKE...

Y-YOU MEAN, THAT MONEY WE KILLED OURSELVES WORKING TO SAVE UP...

MM... GONE. ALL OF IT.
THEY SAY PUNTERS OUGHTA STAY OUT OF THE ADZUKI MARKET, WELL...GUESS THEY KNOW WHAT THEY'RE TALKING ABOUT...

WE'RE STONE BROKE?
MM...THEY PLUCKED THE LAST HAIR OUTTA MY ASS...

SO... WHAT'M I SUPPOSED TO DO WITH THIS BABY?!

WELL ...

HOW'M I SUPPOSED TO RAISE *TWO* CHILDREN IF WE'RE PENNILESS?!
WELL ...

HAANH ...
HAANH ...

GUESS... WE GOT NO CHOICE, THIS TIME ...

HAANH ...
WELL, I'LL BE WORKING LONG, HARD HOURS AGAIN, SO...

I S'POSE... WE'LL HAVE TO...

SHWA
I'LL BE THE BABY'S MOMMY!!
!!

I'LL BE THE BABY'S MOMMY.

HEH?

THE ROLLING STONES, T. REX, JIMI HENDRIX...

DOOM DA DA DOOM

BOP BAM

CREEDENCE CLEARWATER REVIVAL, JOHN LENNON, BOB DYLAN...

DOOM BOOM

GWONK GA GA GA

GYEE GYAA

IF I HAD THAT GUITAR, I COULD BE JUST LIKE THOSE GUYS...

KYUP KYUUN

IF ONLY I HAD THAT WEAPON...

DOOM DA DA DOOM

KENJI.

I TOLD YOU, DON'T JUST OPEN THE DOOR LIKE THAT.

IT'S PAPER. IT'LL RIP IF I KNOCK.

I'LL JUST LEAVE THIS HERE.
LEAVE WHAT THERE?

S... S... S... SIS!!
WH-WH-WHAT THE HECK IS...?!

THAT'S THE ONE YOU WANTED, RIGHT? I'VE SEEN YOU...
AT THAT MUSIC SHOP BY THE STATION, WITH YOUR FACE UP AGAINST THE GLASS.

♡♯♪★!!

THERE'S THIS GUY AT SCHOOL WHO'S REALLY RICH. HE HAS LOTS OF GUITARS.

I LET HIM TAKE ME OUT AND HE GAVE ME THAT.

HE WAS A CREEP, THOUGH.
SHWAP

THUD
THUD
THUD
THUD

THUD
THUD
HEY, DON'T RUN IN THE HOUSE!!

SHWOOSH

WHAT'RE YOU OPENING THE CURTAINS FOR?! THE STORE'S CLOSED!!

FWAP

TUMP

THERE I WAS, REFLECTED IN THE GLASS.
WHAT'RE YOU DOING?!
I SAW A GUY HOLDING A MACHINE GUN...

...AND HE WAS TOTALLY INVINCIBLE.

NOT THAT THERE'S MUCH TO THINK ABOUT.
IF YOUR SALES STAY AS SLUGGISH AS THEY ARE NOW, WE WILL FIND IT IMPOSSIBLE TO RENEW OUR CONTRACT WITH YOU.

IF, HOWEVER, YOU TACKLE THE SOURCE OF THE PROBLEM AND GET RID OF THAT LOAD ON YOUR BACK...

SHE'S NOT A LOAD.
EH?

SHE'S NOT AN OBJECT.
WHAT ARE YOU TRYING TO SAY, MR. ENDO?

HER NAME IS KANNA. SHE'S NOT A THING.

LISTEN HERE, MR. ENDO ...

I'LL INCREASE OUR SALES. I'LL WORK MYSELF DOWN TO THE BONE.
THEN, IF YOU STILL WANT TO CANCEL THE CONTRACT, GO AHEAD. WE'LL GO BACK TO BEING A LIQUOR STORE.

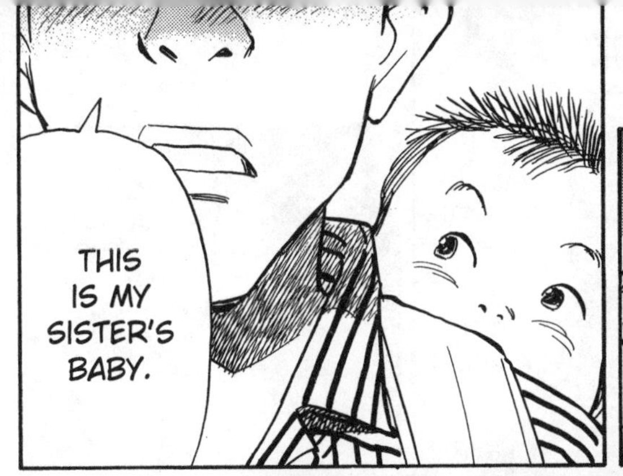
THIS IS MY SISTER'S BABY.

...

AND UNTIL MY SISTER COMES BACK, I'M RAISING HER.

YOU'VE... UH, MADE YOUR POINT, MR. ENDO...

I'LL TAKE IT BACK TO HEAD-QUARTERS FOR CONSIDER-ATION!!
TOK TOK TOK

DAAAA!

WHY'D YOU HAVE TO SAY THAT?!

MM... WELL
THEY CANCEL THE CONTRACT, WE'RE FINISHED!!

MM... IT'LL WORK OUT.

NO, IT'S NOT GOING TO WORK OUT.
YOU'RE A FOOL, IS WHAT YOU ARE!!

So your plan and my plan turn out to be the same. How marvelous, that I was able to meet someone with the same plan as mine.

JUMPED IN FRONT OF A TRAIN...
THOUGH HE REALLY WASN'T THE TYPE TO DO SOME-THING LIKE THAT.

NOBODY COULD BELIEVE IT WHEN IT HAPPENED. IN FACT, SOME PEOPLE WERE SAYING HE MUST'VE BEEN PUSHED FROM BEHIND...

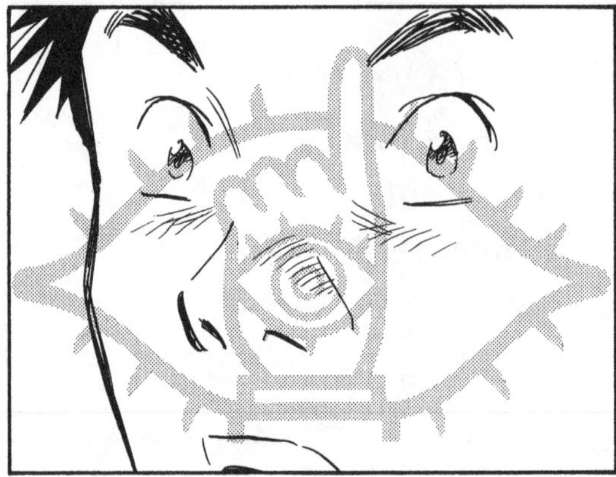

WHUMP

Chapter 9 The Man Behind

I'VE BEEN TRANS-FERRED... I LEAVE THE DAY AFTER TOMOR-ROW.

OH...
WHERE TO?

KUALA LUM-PUR...
THAT'S AWFULLY FAR AWAY...

I... I KNOW I SENT YOU THAT LETTER, BUT...

THE PLANE LEAVES AT 12:30... I RESERVED A SEAT FOR YOU TOO.
I'LL BE WAITING ...

EVEN IF YOU DON'T COME TO THE AIRPORT ...
HERE ...

IT'S MY ADDRESS OVER THERE ...
I'LL BE WAITING FOR YOU...

AL-
WAYS
...
I'LL BE
WAITING
FOR
YOU...

WELL,
THEN
...

新米
入荷しました

GAAA
PHWOOSH

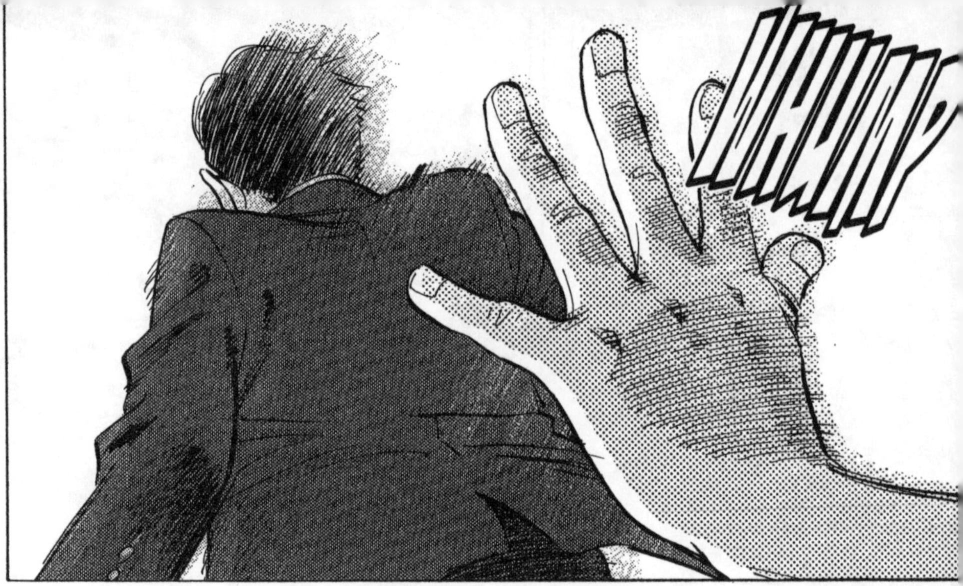

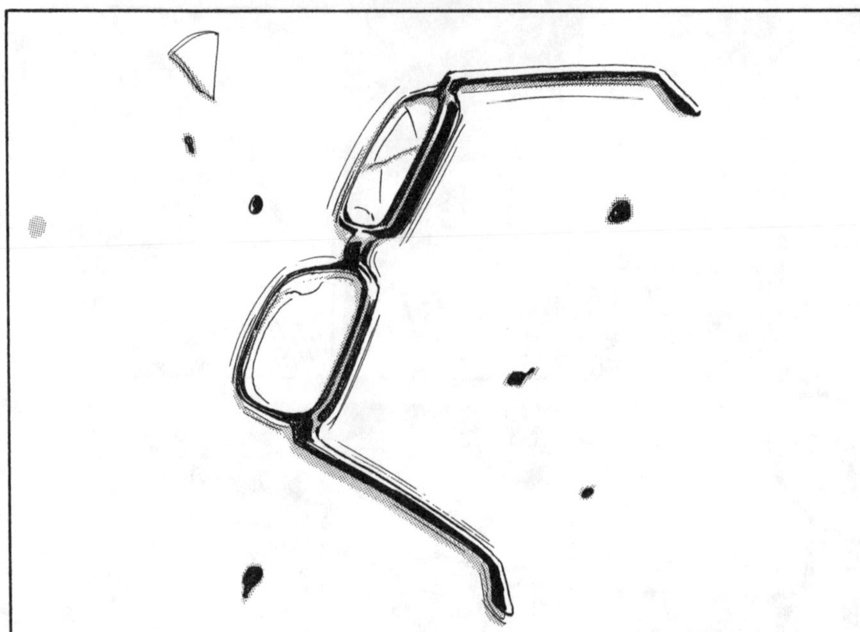

Chapter 9
The Man Behind

HYAAAGH

A SUICIDE!!

SOME-ONE JUMPED UNDER THE TRAIN!!

*Commuter passes sold here.

I-I'M SORRY, BUT WE HAVE NO IDEA RIGHT NOW WHEN SERVICE IS GOING TO BE RESTORED!!

I'VE GOT AN IMPORTANT MEETING! I CAN'T BE LATE!!
I'M SORRY, BUT YOU'LL HAVE TO TAKE THE BUS. FROM THE SOUTH SIDE OF THE STATION!!

HAVE YOU SEEN THE LINES FOR THE BUS?! WE COULD WAIT FOR HOURS!!

I HAVE AN EXAM TODAY!! WHAT'LL I DO IF I MISS IT?!
ARGH, FORGET THIS!!
YOU THINK WE CAN GET A CAB?!

MAN... THIS TOTALLY SUCKS...

SUCH A DRAG... I'VE GOT AN EXAM TOO.

OH, WELL. GUESS I'LL HAVE TO GO BY BIKE...

*Station South Bus Center

...

ARGH
...

RATTLE
RATTLE
DAMMIT. I HATE THIS!!

DON'T WORRY ABOUT IT. MINE'S UNDER THERE TOO...

HEY ...
WHICH ONE'S YOURS?
RATTLE

RATTLE
OH... THANK YOU.

UH... THAT ONE.
SO, DID YOU MAKE IT TO YOUR EXAM THE OTHER DAY?
RATTLE

MORE OR LESS ...
I WAS 20 MINUTES LATE.

WELL, I PRETTY MUCH GOT TO MINE ON TIME, BUT...
RATTLE

...I'D TOTALLY STUDIED THE WRONG PAGES SO I WAS, LIKE, CLUELESS.
LIKE, SAME DIFFER-ENCE IF I'D TOTALLY MISSED IT.

ME TOO.

FOR REAL?

HA HA HA HA HA!

THERE YOU GO.
THANK YOU.

YOU WOULDN'T WANT TO...
...HAVE SOME COFFEE WITH ME.

SURE.

FOR REAL?

JUST FOR A LITTLE WHILE. MY DAD GETS ON MY CASE IF I'M LATE...
COOL! LET'S MAKE IT A BURGER, THEN!!

SO, JUST FOLLOW THESE STEPS. ARE YOU QUITE SURE ABOUT THIS?

OF COURSE.
IT DOESN'T HAVE TO BE YOU TO WORK?

GETTING A WOMAN TO FALL FOR YOU IS A PIECE OF CAKE.

DO YOU THINK OUR FRIEND WILL BE SUCCESSFUL TOO?

DEFINITELY. OUR FRIEND WILL BE SO MUCH BETTER AT IT THAN I AM.

AND ANYWAY, SHE'S REALLY VULNERABLE RIGHT NOW. SHE JUST LOST THE MAN SHE LOVED, RIGHT?
WOMEN LIKE THAT ARE THE EASIEST. TRUST ME.

BECOMING A TRUE "FRIEND" IS A THOUSAND TIMES HARDER.

YOU YOURSELF, THOUGH, ARE SLOWLY STARTING TO EXPERIENCE ONENESS WITH THE COSMOS, ARE YOU NOT?
WELL... THE DEEPER I GET, THE MORE I REALIZE HOW GREAT OUR FRIEND TRULY IS.

OUR FRIEND HAS A VERY HIGH OPINION OF YOU.
OH, GOOD ...

IF OUR FRIEND IS HAPPY WITH ME, THAT'S ALL THAT MATTERS.

IT TOOK A LOT OF COURAGE TO DO WHAT YOU DID.
NO IT DIDN'T ...

A TRAIN STATION AT RUSH HOUR...

I JUST GAVE HIM A LITTLE SHOVE.

NOT MANY PEOPLE COULD'VE DONE THAT. NOT EVEN FOR THEIR FRIEND.

THAT'S WHAT I WANTED TO BE-- A KILLER.

THE GOOD GUYS ARE ALWAYS SO SQUARE. YOU KNOW, ALL THOSE GUNG-HO TV AND MANGA HEROES?

WELL, EVER SINCE I WAS A KID...

THE BAD GUYS ARE ALWAYS THE COOL ONES.

BUT ON TV, THE BAD GUYS ALWAYS GET KILLED AT THE END.

THIS ISN'T TV.
THIS IS REALITY.

OOPS ...

SORRY, BUT I BETTER GO HOME ...

CUZ OF YOUR DAD?
YEAH ...

WHAT'S YOUR DAD DO? WORK-WISE.

IT'S TOO EMBAR-RASSING TO TELL YOU.

NO WAY, WHAT?
WELL, HE'S ON TV SOMETIMES. ON THE EDUCATIONAL CHANNEL ...

YOU EVER SEE A PROFESSOR NAMED SHIKI-SHIMA?

YOU KNOW WHAT, I NEVER WATCH THAT CHANNEL.
SO WHAT DOES HE TEACH, ANY-WAY?

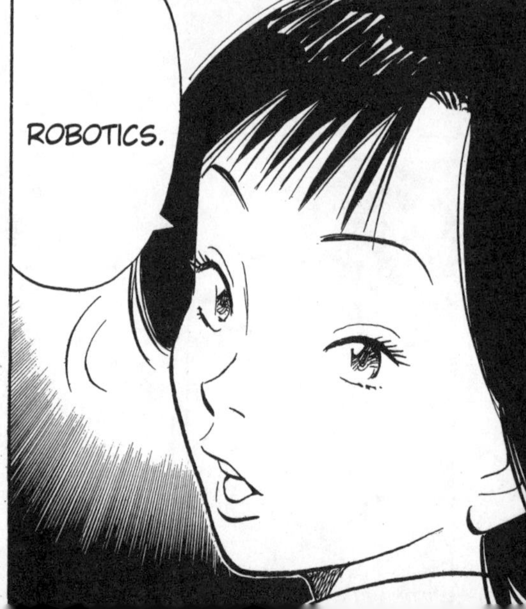
ROBOTICS.

KREE
KREE
KREE

ZWOOON
ZWOOON
KREE
KREE
KREE
KRASH

THE...UN-IDENTIFIED OBJECT IS NOW HEADING TOWARD SHINJUKU!!
CLOSE OFF KOSHU HIGHWAY AND MEIJI AVENUE! WE'RE ON MAXIMUM SECURITY ALERT!!
WOOOOO
KLANG
KLANG
KLANG
KLANG
WE NEED MORE PEOPLE! SEND IN REINFORCE-MENTS A.S.A.P!!
DECEMBER 2000

Chapter 10 The Prophet

THE FIRST TIME I EVER SET FOOT IN A COFFEE SHOP WAS ON THE WAY HOME FROM SEEING SON OF GODZILLA WITH MY SISTER AT THE KOKUSAI THEATER IN FRONT OF THE STATION.

NO?

OF COURSE NOT! GODZILLA'S GOT TO BE A ***MALE***.

* Yanagiya Kingoro: Actor and comedian who gained widespread popularity through such TV comedies as *Gesture*. Died in 1972.

YOU'RE RIGHT.
IT IS STRANGE THERE WAS NO PARTNER.

PART-NER?

WHAD-DAYA MEAN, PARTNER?
A FATHER GOD-ZILLA.

A *FATHER* GOD-ZILLA?
BUT THERE'S ONLY ONE GODZILLA.

YOU CAN'T HAVE A BABY WITH JUST ONE.

HUH?

?
?

WELL, WE CAN'T HAVE IT.

SITTING AT THE NEXT TABLE WAS THE YOUNG COUPLE WHO'D MOVED INTO AN APARTMENT NEAR OUR HOUSE.

"LIVING IN SIN" SOUNDED PRETTY SEXY, EVEN TO AN EIGHT-YEAR-OLD ...
HEY...IT'S OKAY. WHY DON'T WE... GO TO THE DOCTOR TO FIND OUT... OKAY?

I DIDN'T SAY ANY-THING ABOUT HAVING IT...I JUST SAID I'M LATE...
WE'RE BROKE ENOUGH AS IT IS...

I'D HEARD MY MOM GOSSIPING ABOUT THEM. SHE SAID THEY WERE "LIVING IN SIN."

Bar
LONDON

MY FIRST COFFEE SHOP FELT LIKE A VERY GROWN-UP KIND OF PLACE.

NEXT DOOR, THERE WAS A BAR CALLED "LONDON."

LONDON
KREE
Closed

!!

WHAT IS IT, LITTLE BOY?

UH... NOTHING!!
WE'RE GOING, KENJI.
UH... YEAH.
I SUDDENLY HAD A PICTURE OF MYSELF WHEN I WAS GROWN UP-- I'D LIVE IN SIN ...

...AND GO TO THE COFFEE SHOP "SAN FRANCISCO," AND FREQUENT THE BAR "LONDON"...
Coffee shop
SAN FRANCISCO
Bar
LONDON

1997
U.S. Gripped with Fear!!
Over 50 Dead with Death Toll Rising!!
Mystery Microbe Hits San Francisco

WE DON'T WORK OUR ASSES OFF, THEY'RE GONNA CANCEL OUR CONTRACT!!

DAAAAA!!

Chapter 10 The Prophet

HANH
DRIP
DRIP
HANH
HANH
DRIP

KA-THUNK

WHATSA MATTER, HEI-CHAN?
THERE'S SOMEBODY IN MY HOUSE.

POKE POKE
HEY.
HEY, YOU, COME ON OUT.

HANH
HANH
HANH

WHAT'RE YOU DOIN' IN THERE? COME OUT.
YA CAN'T JUST WALK INTA SOME-BODY'S HOUSE LIKE THAT.

HANH
HANH

UH-OH. GUY'S BEEN STABBED.
THIS AIN'T THE KINDA GUEST WE WANT COMIN' FOR A VISIT.

HEY, YOU OKAY?
YOU GONNA DIE, DON'T DO IT HERE.

YOU GOT ANY MONEY?
YOU GOT HEALTH INSUR-ANCE?

HANH
N-NO ...
HANH

WHAT NOW?
GUESS WE CALL 119 FOR AN AMBU-LANCE?

N-NO! D-DON'T !!

BUT IF WE DON'T ...
LOOK, YOU GONNA DIE, DO IT SOME-PLACE ELSE.

I...I WAS... LOOK-ING... FOR...

SH-SHOULD BE... AROUND HERE...
YOUR DOG RUN AWAY?

FOR WHAT?
YOU LOSE YOUR WALLET?

KENJI...
THE... GREAT... KENJI...

KENJI?

THAT'S THE FELLOW AT THAT KING MART.
OH... KAMI-SAMA.

SO HE'S BEING SUMMONED TO ACTION, AFTER ALL...

AFTER ALL?
YOU DREAMED THIS WOULD HAPPEN?

SORT OF.
I DON'T THINK THAT GUY'S UP TO THE TASK, THOUGH ...

WELL, I'LL GO GET HIM ANYWAY.
IF HE'LL COME, THAT IS...

CHU-SAN, YOU'RE A FAST RUNNER, AREN'T YOU.

?

酒

*Liquor

...

PICK WHATEVER YOU WANT, CHU-SAN.
HUH? YOU SURE? THIS YOUR TREAT, KAMI-SAMA?

JUST GO AHEAD, PICK ONE.
GEE, THANKS.

I'LL TAKE THIS GINGER-FRIED PORK LUNCH!! THANKS!
HO, THAT'S A GOOD ONE.

NOW, RUN.
HUH?

WHAT... THE HELL DO YA MEAN?

ACCORDING TO WHAT I DREAMED, YOU DON'T RUN NOW, YOU DIE LIKE A DOG LATER.

THAT OKAY WITH YOU?
WHA--?

NOW, GO!!
HYA...

HYAAAAARGH!!
DA
HEY!!

COME BACK HERE, YOU! STOP, THIEF!!
HYEEEEEE!!

KEEP RUNNING, CHU-SAN!! DON'T GET CAUGHT UNTIL YOU GET TO HEI-CHAN'S!!
HUH?!

YOU TOO, SONNY. IF YOU WANT TO SAVE THE WORLD, GO AFTER HIM!!

HUNH ?!

HURRY UP! YOUR THIEF THERE'S GETTING AWAY!!
ARGH !!

SLOW DOWN, CHU-SAN!! I KNEW THIS FELLA WAS NOTHING TO WRITE HOME ABOUT!!
?
?
HYEEEEE!!

HFF
HFF
HFF

GIVE... ME THAT... GINGER-FRIED PORK LUNCH!!
NO! I HAND THIS OVER, I DIE LIKE A DOG!!
WHEEZE
WHEEZE

HFF
HFF
THAT'S HIM. THAT'S KENJI.
?

YOU'RE KENJI?
HUH ?!
DO SOME-THING ABOUT THIS GUY.

GWUMP
HUH... WHA--?
WARGH!!

WHO'RE ...
...YOU ...

THIS IS HIM. KENJI.

YOU?

TH-THIS ...
...DOPEY-LOOKING CLOWN... IS... KOFF KOFF

HEY... WAIT A MINUTE!! THIS GUY'S HURT!!
IT'S OKAY, IT'S OKAY.
BUT, HE'S *REALLY* HURT!!

C-COULD A...GUY LIKE YOU... REALLY BE... THE GREAT PROPHET?!

HUNH ?!

I... RISKED MY LIFE...
...TO ESCAPE FROM THERE... TO LET YOU KNOW...

LET... ME KNOW... WHAT?

WHAT'S HE GONNA DO NEXT?!

HUNH ?!
I'M ASKING YOU, WHAT COMES NEXT?!

THEY SCATTERED GERMS ALL OVER SAN FRANCISCO ...
WHERE NEXT?!

I...

I DON'T UNDER-STAND!! WHAT THE HELL'S HE TALKING ABOUT?!

DON'T PLAY DUMB WITH ME!!
HYARGH!!

KOFF KOFF
I BE-LIEVED... FOR A LONG TIME...

I BELIEVED... IT WAS...A WONDERFUL GROUP...

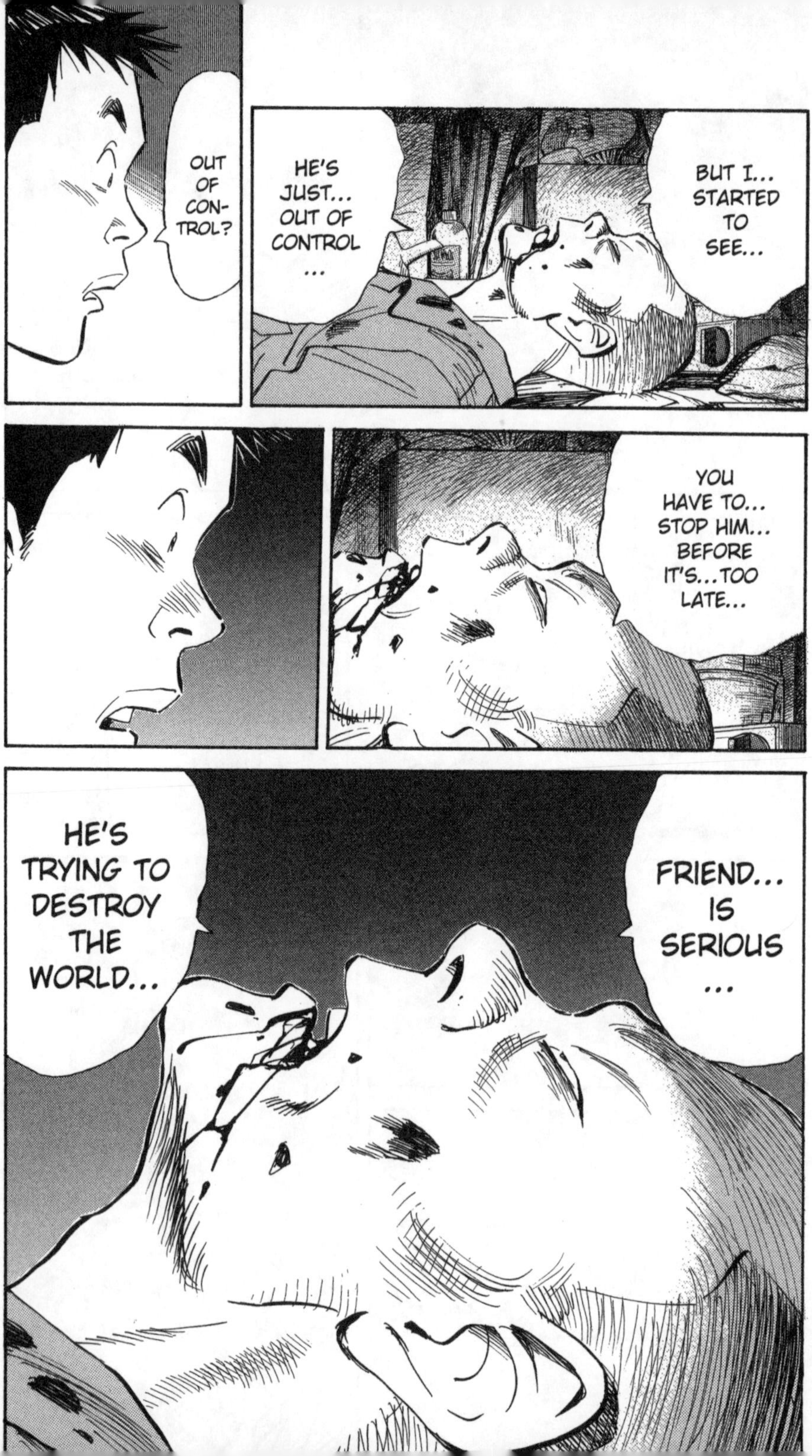

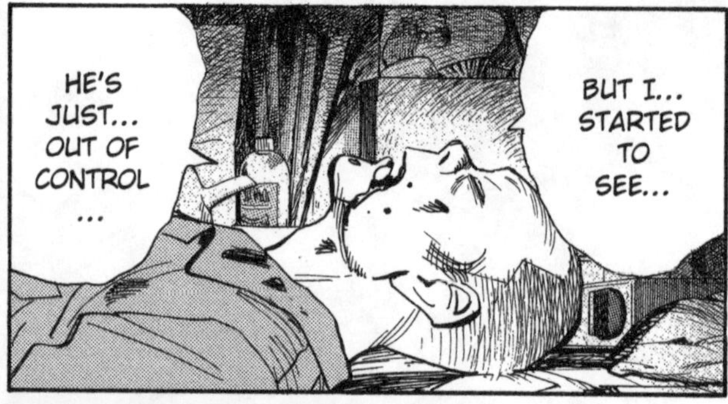

FRIEND... IS SERIOUS ...

HE'S TRYING TO DESTROY THE WORLD...

FRIEND
...

SO WHO EXACTLY IS THIS "FRIEND" YOU'RE TALKING ABOUT?

YOU KNOW
...

YOU KNOW WHO HE IS
...
YOU KNOW EVERY-THING
...

I'M TELLING YOU, I DON'T!!

IT'S ALL... YOUR IDEA. YOU CAME UP WITH IT.
HUH?

THIS IS ALL SOMETHING YOU THOUGHT UP WHEN YOU WERE A KID, ISN'T IT?

Chapter 11 Open Your Eyes!!

READ ALL THE MANGA YOU WANT!!
EAT AS MUCH FOOD AS YOU WANT!!

YEAH, AND YOU DON'T HAVE TO DO ALL THE STUFF YOU *DON'T* WANNA DO...

IT'S LIKE HAVING SUMMER VACATION EVERY DAY.
YEAH, BUT WITH-OUT THE HOME-WORK.

PRETTY NICE, HUH? BEING MASTERS OF THE WORLD.

YEAH!

HEY, WAIT A MINUTE !!
THAT'S NOT THE STORY WE'RE WRITING, YOU GUYS!!

WE'RE TRYING TO FIGURE OUT HOW TO SAVE THE WORLD *FROM* THE LEAGUE OF EVIL!!

IMAGINE EATING ALL YOU WANT!
I KNOW, BUT THE LEAGUE OF EVIL'S STARTING TO SOUND PRETTY GOOD.

WHAT'RE YOU TALKING ABOUT?! EVIL'S ALWAYS DESTROYED IN THE END!!

AL-WAYS?
IF THE BAD GUYS DROP AN H-BOMB, ALL THE GOOD GUYS WILL BE DESTROYED.

THEY WON'T USE AN H-BOMB.

IF THEY DROP AN H-BOMB, ALL THE BUILDINGS AND EVERY-THING WILL BE RUINED.
THEN WHAT'S THEIR PLAN OF ATTACK, OTCHO?

GERM WAR-FARE.

GERM WAR-FARE?

OH YEAH, MY SISTER WAS SAYING ...
...THERE'S ALL KINDS OF SCARY GERMS OUT THERE.

LIKE TYPHUS GERMS, AND CHOLERA GERMS, AND DYSENTERY GERMS.
SO WHAT, THE BAD GUYS ATTACK WHEN EVERYONE'S SICK WITH DIARRHEA?

THAT SOUNDS REALLY STINKY.
WE CAN'T SAVE THE WORLD IF WE'RE SICK WITH DIARRHEA.

OKAY!!
THE LEAGUE OF EVIL WILL ATTACK USING GERM WARFARE... THERE.

WHERE DO THEY ATTACK FIRST?
TOKYO?

TOKYO'S LAST.

THE STORY'S TAKING PLACE IN JAPAN. IF THEY ATTACK TOKYO FIRST, THE WHOLE THING'S OVER ALREADY.

SO... CAN YOU THINK OF SOME-PLACE?
YEAH!

SAN FRANCISCO!!

SAN FRANCIS-CO?

YOU KNOW, THERE'S THAT PLACE NEAR THE MOVIE THEATER. THE COFFEE SHOP "SAN FRANCISCO."

YOU'RE PICKING THEIR TARGET FROM A COFFEE SHOP?
SO OKAY, WHERE DO THEY ATTACK NEXT?
FIRST IT WAS SAN FRANCISCO ...
WHERE NEXT?
WHOOOSH
YOU THOUGHT THIS UP AS A KID, RIGHT?
WHERE ARE THEY GONNA SCATTER THE GERMS NEXT?

WHOOSH
Coffee shop
SAN FRANCISCO
Bar
LONDON
LON...

1997
LONDON
...
Chapter 11
Open Your Eyes!!

SO IT WAS YOU...
YOU'RE THE ONE WHO...

N-NO, BUT THAT WAS ...

YOU CAME UP WITH IT... HOW ELSE WOULD YOU KNOW IT'S LONDON IF YOU DIDN'T?
WHY? WHY LONDON ...

I CAN'T TELL YOU...
IT'S TOO STUPID ...

AND THIS ...
THIS WAS... YOUR IDEA TOO...
KA-CHAK

HUH?
WHAT IS THIS ...

HEY
...
WATCH
IT...

A...
LASER
GUN?

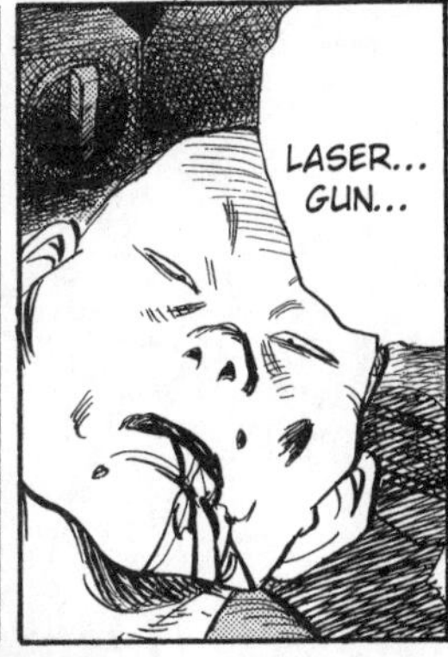
LASER...
GUN...

THAT'S STILL A
PILOT MODEL...
DON'T TRY
SHOOTING IT...
!!

YOU
THOUGHT
THAT UP
TOO...
DIDN'T
YOU...

...

WHO IS IT...
WHO'S THIS "FRIEND" OF YOURS?

IT WASN'T JUST ME...
I'M NOT THE ONLY ONE WHO CAME UP WITH THAT STORY...

IT'S OTCHO, ISN'T IT?

OTCHO'S THE ONE WHO THOUGHT THIS UP WITH ME...
IT'S OCHIAI CHOJI, ISN'T IT?

I DON'T KNOW ...

HE WAS ALWAYS JUST OUR "FRIEND" ...
WE REALLY BELIEVED IT TOO...
THAT HE WAS OUR FRIEND ...

WE BELIEVED ...
...HE WAS A TRUE PROPHET ...

THE TRUE SAVIOR ...

BUT... EVER SINCE THAT TIME...
MY DOUBTS... STARTED SPREADING LIKE A STAIN...

THAT TIME?

AND THAT STAIN JUST KEPT GROWING ...
...BIGGER AND BIGGER ...

WOULD A PERSON WHO'S ABOUT TO DIE... TELL A LIE?
I STARTED WONDERING...IF MAYBE... WHAT HE SAID WAS TRUE...

WHO?

RIGHT BEFORE... I PUSHED HIM OVER... HE SAID...

PUSHED?
BEFORE YOU PUSHED ***WHO*** OVER?

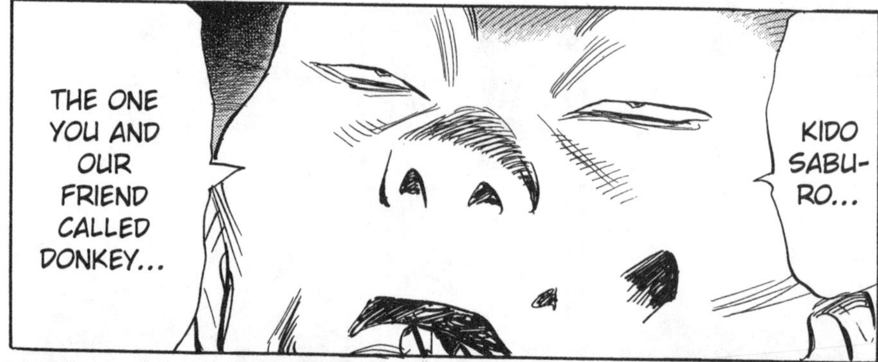
KIDO SABURO...
THE ONE YOU AND OUR FRIEND CALLED DONKEY...

WHOOSH

OPEN YOUR EYES!!
YOU'RE BEING DECEIVED!!
WHOOSH
YOUR FRIEND IS NO SAVIOR!!
EVERY-THING YOUR FRIEND IS SAYING...

...ALL OF IT...WAS THOUGHT UP BY KENJI WHEN WE WERE KIDS!!

OPEN ... YOUR...

THUNK

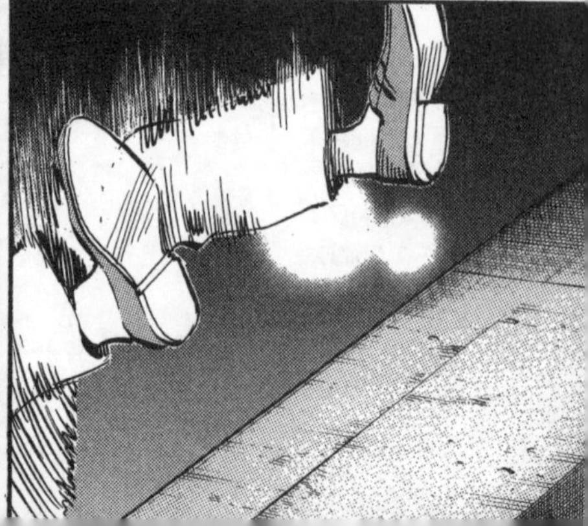

DONKEYYYYY!!

YOU'RE THE ONLY ONE WHO CAN STOP HIM...

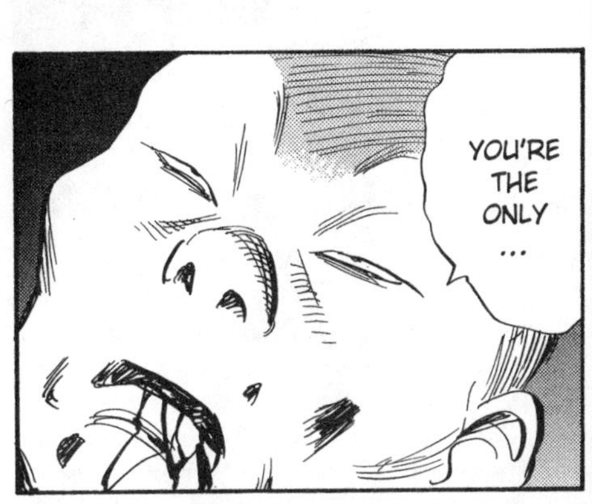

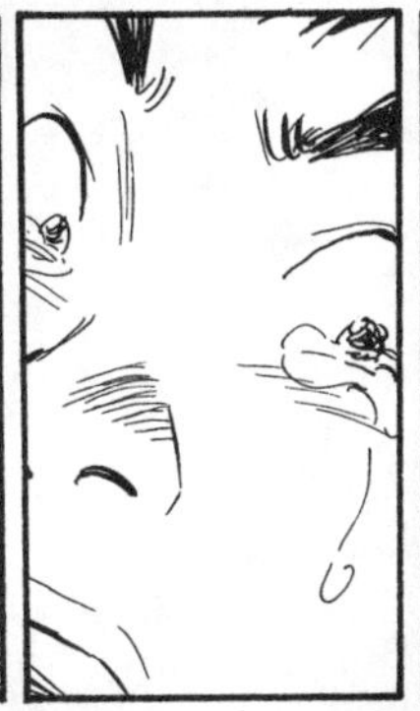

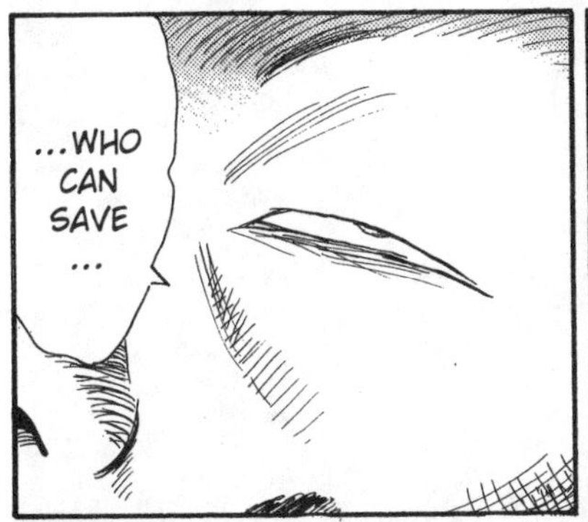

KA- TUNK

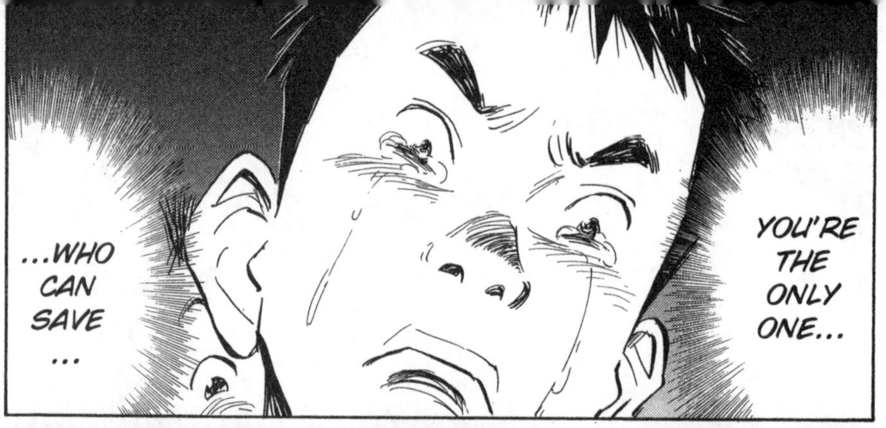

...THE WORLD ...

TO BE CONTINUED